pet loss

A Spiritual Guide

Julia A. Harris

Lant
A Div.   Jl booklight Inc.

2002
Lantern Books
One Union Square West, Suite 201
New York, NY 10003

Printed in the United States of America

Cover photograph by Amy K. Pickering

Library of Congress Cataloging-in-Publication Data

Harris, Julia A., 1970–
 Pet loss : a spiritual guide / by Julia A. Harris.
   p. cm.
Includes bibliographical references (p.   ).
 ISBN 1-59056-028-0 (alk. paper)
  1. Pet owners—Psychology. 2. Pets—Death—Psychological aspects. 3.
Bereavement—Psychological aspects. 4. Funeral rites and ceremonies.
5. Pet owners—Religious life. I. Title.
 SF411.47 .H375 2002
 155.9'37—dc21

                                                        2002008901

*In memory of my beloved Miniature Spitz,
Sasha, who died of cancer.*

Acknowledgments

I WOULD LIKE TO THANK ABBEY GLEN PET MEMORIAL PARK AND Pleasant Plains Crematorium in Lafayette, New Jersey for the teachings that evolved my knowledge of both people and their pets.

Table of Contents

Introduction

HOW LUCKY WE ARE TO LIVE UPON THIS BEAUTIFUL EARTH, surrounded by such a variety of living creatures, each with his or her own personality. Like people, animals capture our interest, wonderment and love by sharing their individual, unique traits and behaviors. No action is more rewarding than becoming a pet guardian to one or more animals. Pet guardians place all selfish needs aside to provide another creature with food, shelter, love and devotion. We adore the animals—whether domestic or wild—who coax our inner child outward by their presence. We talk to them, worry about them, and place their well-being above even our own.

Many of you probably had family pets when growing up, or have a pet at this time with whom you share a special, loving relationship. Perhaps you have faced the emotional distress of coping with the death of a beloved pet. I have experienced the grief of pet loss many times along with the joy of having an animal companion as a part of my family in life. It is difficult to accept that animals do not live as long as humans, and those of us who have been touched by the devotion and unconditional love of a pet feel robbed when our treasured companion is suddenly gone from our life. Although we will always remember and love our deceased pets and cherish the bond we shared, at their death we face extreme emotional upset that has been too rarely acknowledged in our society. Now pet loss and pet death are gaining new attention in the mental health professions. The grief of these experiences is real and intense, and calls out for the kind of help that is offered in this book.

My fascination with and love of animals started in early childhood, when my mother and I would adopt stray cats. As an adult, I have picked up dogs or cats wandering aimlessly along the roadside. Caring for and loving my own animals has never been enough; I advocate for animal rights and welfare because there are so many wild and domestic animals who are abused and exploited and desperately need someone to be their voice.

This devotion to animals led to my involvement with the Pet Adoption League, one of the largest animal rescue organizations in New Jersey. I experienced years of fulfillment rescuing, fostering and preserving the lives of countless abused, neglected and homeless animals. This experience prompted me to pursue a career as a pet bereavement counselor at a New Jersey pet cemetery. At the same time, I attended human and pet psychology courses. I studied the human-animal bond and pet bereavement to better equip myself to assist grieving pet lovers, and I learned to deal with the phases of grief over the loss of a pet. My studies, however, could not have prepared me for the interactions that lay ahead. People react to death in different ways, and experiencing these reactions firsthand was a most valuable education.

In my counseling, I encountered many religions, philosophies and personalities. I helped religious individuals find comfort in their beliefs, and for others, I turned to world philosophical and religious ideas. I believe that it is important for everyone to have a system for coping with loss and achieving resolution that speaks directly from personal religious beliefs. This benefits the grieving process and uplifts the breaking heart. My own spiritual practices have been influenced by many religions, such as Christianity, Buddhism, and Lakota. From each I've taken enlightening beliefs that continue to shape my understanding of the physical and spiritual worlds. Each has lent its influence to the rituals in this book.

The greatest triumph of my many years of helping both animals and people is this opportunity to share the knowledge I've gained through my experiences. In this book, you'll find not only a step-by-step guide to dealing with the emotions called forth by a pet's death, but also detailed information on making final arrangements for your pet. You'll learn the best ways to explain pet death to grieving children and to unsympathetic adults who may not understand your sorrow. Various religious beliefs are explored, and rituals and meditations included, to help you heal and cope with your loss. And you'll find ample support for what all animal lovers know: that the human-pet bond is one of deep love and sharing, and that mourning a deceased pet is a normal, positive process.

You are not alone—there are countless individuals like you and me who have walked the path of sorrow. Together we travel a twisting emotional and psychological way that will lead to resolution. Through this book I hope to create a living memorial not only to my own very special pets but to yours as well.

1

The Human and Pet Bond

To FULLY COMPREHEND THE LASTING EXISTENCE OF THE HUMAN and pet bond, we must consider the history of prehistoric humankind. We have all seen pictures of the cave carvings and symbols depicting human beings at hunt, at feast, and at rest side by side with animal companions. We may think of the intricate Egyptian statues and art that convey such fascination with and love of the various species of the animal kingdom. Through history we find evidence of animals earning a place as pets by somehow helping humanity—such as the cats' role in saving Europe from the plague. Ancient civilizations such as Egypt and Sumer venerated certain animals and gave them a role in religious and magical practices; in Egypt, for example, cats were regarded as sacred. From the pet dogs of famous kings and rulers to the ancient shepherds' herding dogs, it is evident that since the birth of humanity we've found working and loving relationships with the creatures who surround us. Animals have shared the company of our earliest ancestors and undoubtedly will be companions to our future generations.

The interaction of human and animal did not arise from mere accident or simple need; it was a natural process of mutual interest of both human and beast. Perhaps it began with a beast drawing near to a prehistoric fire in search of food, and a human feeling moved to share the hunted meal with the animal, who eventually became a protector. It can be imagined that the early bond between human and animal soon evolved into a strong relationship of devotion and love. It may have seemed to humankind that the beasts sharing the earth served a much greater purpose than assistance at daily activities of hunt and survival. Animals extended unconditional love, enriched the lives of family members, and displayed a playful friendliness that made them welcome company.

Relationships with Pets

Humans have a basic need to provide love and nurturing—not only to each other and to offspring, but also to the surrounding world. Though this need may not always be apparent, each of us has it and acts on it in some way. We see this demonstrated in the activities of children, who provide nurturing care to their dolls, toys, friends and family. Adults exhibit similar traits with their children, friends, spouses and pets. The pet fulfills a crucial purpose in our human lives.

It is impossible to express in words the joy we feel in caring for a companion animal. Not only do pets offer us unconditional love and company, but they show us an innocent, pure dependence we haven't experienced since earliest childhood. We respond to this gift with feelings of love that seem infinite. Our bond with our pets allows us to share all the trials of life with another creature.

When the worries and frustrations of daily life trouble our minds, our pet nudges at our body to give comfort and a form of understanding. Our pets are capable of sensing our distress, anger and a variety of emotions, and they wish to help us in any way possible. Our tainted emotional responses to a hectic life within a chaotic society fade into nothingness as we share serene, loving time alone with our beloved pet.

In interaction with out pets we are our true selves. There is no need to display the false corporate flair necessary for the career at the office. No matter how the rest of the world may react to us, a pet thoroughly accepts each of us, without passing judgment. A pet's obedience makes us feel successful as individuals, and his or her respect gives us self-esteem and self-worth we may rarely experience elsewhere.

The human-pet bond, with its ever-evolving exchange of intimate enrichment, is unlike any other in the entire universe. It is as if the gods placed animals upon this earth to live in harmony and love with humanity, to share a divine relationship purer than most we experience in the course of our lives.

Our appreciation for our pets' efforts, respect and love unfolds in the way we treat them as our most cherished companions. Some individuals term their pet "my child" or "my best friend." Often, adults will refer to themselves as their pet's "mom" or "dad," and children will refer to their pet as a sibling or best buddy. Individuals may spend grocery money on extra dog toys when FiFi already has the pleasure of twenty play toys, or trade in a trip to the hair salon to have their suffering Sheba flea dipped. As we would do for a relative or dearest friend, we do whatever it takes to return the love pets give us.

Touching Our Pets

We cuddle and pet our devoted companions with total freedom. By physically showing us that they find great pleasure in our attention, they reassure us when we wonder if they truly love and understand us. In our relationships with human friends, however, touching is usually discouraged or seen as somehow wrong. Couples often shy away from displaying their affection in front of other people. Perhaps it is due in part to this customary restraint that we so eagerly touch and caress our pets—affectionate displays that are, ironically, readily accepted in human society. How many people have you seen driving their cars with the family dog in the front seat and the spouse or children in the back? How many times have you witnessed the affectionate "head kiss" guardians give their pets in private or in public? This behavior is enormously enriching for us emotionally. It has been medically proven that we lower our blood pressure, improve our heartbeat, heighten our resistance to disease and ease our tension, among other tangible benefits, when we caress our pets.[1]

The Human Role in Mutual Bonding

The role we humans play in the human-pet bond is a role born of responsibility. Like the raising of a healthy child, our decision to have a pet carries with it a certain set of obligations. Pets depend upon the care of human companions for as long as they live. They will never become independent as children do. Your role as care provider to your pets strengthens the bond you form with them. Your ministrations to your pets relieve you from daily pressures, grant you joy in their presence, and allow a mutual exchange of love and pleasure. You also gain a sense of security, importance and self-worth; your pet believes in you, needs you and loves you.

It is important to note, however, that the roles some pet guardians assume may be unhealthy. Sensitive care is not harmful, but some individuals go too far by considering themselves true "parents" of a "child" pet, dressing their pets up, giving them infant toys or a stroller to ride in, or putting them through unnecessary and excruciating hygienic procedures. These individuals truly mean no harm; in fact, they are certain they are behaving in the best interest of their pet. Sadly, this is not the case. It is impossible to know for certain if the pet likes or dislikes the excessive physical attention or being made to do child-like activities. There is a concern, however, that the guardian may be losing touch with reality and the relationship may become pathological.

While too much attention may be harmful, too little attention certainly is. We each know of someone who owns a pet and is not responsible—a situation that pains and angers sensitive pet guardians. We wonder why the person even bothered to adopt a pet at all, and why he or she does not give the pet away to a better home. Many of us are moved to volunteer for animal rescue groups to help such neglected animals.

The most reliable pet guardians accept total responsibility for our pet's happiness, physical comfort and health. Our efforts are filled with the best of human love. However, we must all someday face the painful truth that all our love and sensitivity cannot protect our pets from every single danger. When accident, illness or death intrudes in spite of our best efforts, most pet guardians inevitably suffer unnecessary guilt and feel that they have failed to provide responsible care. Yet the circumstances surrounding the death of a pet can truly be out of our control or impossible to anticipate. One of the most important messages I hope you'll take from this book is that this guilt must be recognized and dealt with if resolution is to be achieved.

Our Role Continues in Pet Death

When a pet dies you know intellectually that it is part of a natural cycle; the Wheel of Life turns for all existence. Practically, there are ways to prepare through advance consideration and planning. Emotionally, however, you can never be truly ready. Not knowing for certain what happens at death causes anxiety and sorrow when a person or animal dies. We do not understand death and therefore have difficulty accepting it. Yet at the death of a beloved pet, your responsibility does not end. You must cherish your memories and continue with your life. You will need to accept that your life must go on without your pet, at least on the physical plane, and to care for yourself in a way that will enable you to cope. Somehow, the loss must be endured.

In addition to the time, effort and expense of making final arrangements for your pet, you feel an inner demand to preserve your pet's memory in a positive manner. I have done so by placing the decorative urn containing the ashes of my cat Lester upon a handmade memorial shelf in our living room. Much like the religious rituals we conduct to obtain spiritual enlightenment, memorializing a beloved pet is a healthy step in the grieving process.

Happy memories of your pet can brighten a life that has been shattered by his or her loss. In this book I'll encourage you to remember the enriching experiences that you and your pet shared during his or her lifetime. I'll help you direct your energies toward reminiscences of your joy and mutual love, instead of dwelling on the inevitable loss of your pet.

Pet Dependency

The familiar term "man's best friend" hints at a relationship between humans and pets that transcends by far our interactions with other humans. We enjoy being adored for who we really are by our pets. We unfold ourselves in complete openness to them, and enjoy in return a tremendous loyalty, trust, honesty and security that go beyond what we can obtain from human friends, family, and even lovers or spouses.

There are pet lovers who have forsaken interhuman relationships for the sense of love and security a pet can provide.[2] Sometimes relationships with people can scar us in such a way that we seek out an intimate bond with animals and nature instead. The emotional upset and hurt of not being accepted by the people surrounding us may cause us to adhere to the sanctuary that nature unconditionally provides us and the trusting love we receive from animals. In the case of a troubled marriage or a conflict between family members, one person may focus upon the pet in order to enjoy the comfort of a trouble-free relationship and to receive the support and love that are missing from the human relationship.

Psychologists feel that in some cases people who depend upon their pet so intensely and extend their private selves exclusively to their pet are acting inappropriately. When the world and other people are too threatening, condemning or painful, these individuals isolate themselves in an inner world inhabited by themselves and their pet alone. Social interaction with other people become handicapped by the extreme dependency upon a pet for support.

To lead a fulfilling and productive life we must love and care not only for our pets, but also for ourselves and other people. Although we adore our pets, it is important that we be able to function socially with other humans, resolve conflicts with them and not rely too heavily on our special companions. Such reliance is psychologically unhealthy, especially if one becomes a social recluse. Having estranged ourselves from other people, the loss of a pet is more difficult to deal with than if we had the support of understanding people.

When a pet becomes lost or dies suddenly, the shock and the new void in the dependent person's life can lead to serious mental health issues, an inability to function properly in daily activities and social situations, and even physical illness. If the pet's death is gradual and expected, the dependent individual will dwell exclusively upon the pet's health and upcoming departure, leading to despair and depression that can last beyond the pet's death and may never be resolved.

Almost without exception, grief responses are most extreme when the bereaved has very few or no close human companions.[3] In the absence of human understanding, the love for a pet grows to an abnormal intensity at the time of mourning. It can eventually prove disastrous when everyday coping is privately done in a retreat of suffering, a personal safe haven. Usually the bereaved truly feels that drowning himself or herself in the lost relationship is perfectly justified and even helpful, but this behavior actually makes the grieving process more difficult once reality catches up.

During my work as a pet bereavement counselor I had to counsel and prepare a funeral arrangement for an older woman's pet, a Doberman pinscher. Her children had grown up and moved away, starting families of their own. Her older husband seemed unable to give much, instead exhausting her precious energies and emotions with his selfish demands. When this woman's dog died suddenly of natural causes, her only security in life was gone. Without the love and support of her husband, and without sympathetic friends, this woman went into a state of shock, emotional turmoil and intense pain.

Her health immediately became poor. In my work with her to plan burial arrangements for her beloved dog, I could clearly see that she needed professional help beyond my training as a counselor. I recommended a few therapists and support groups, which she refused. She did not like most people and wanted to mourn alone. In the days before the burial she would call me, sobbing and obviously on the verge of a mental breakdown. I would spend as much time on the telephone with her as needed, to be certain she received support and knew that at least someone was there for her and understood her pain.

On the day of the funeral I met the couple in the wake parlor, where the prepared Doberman pinscher awaited them inside a closed casket. I held the woman, and we talked. Her husband stood carelessly across the room and glanced at his watch impatiently. I counseled her gently before the lifting of the casket lid. Once the lid was raised, I promptly and politely exited the room.

I had been waiting inside my office for a few moments when suddenly the husband threw open the office door and begged my assistance. The woman had gone into hysterics, convinced that her dog was alive. She claimed that he had looked at her (his eyes were closed) and moved his leg. The woman was literally ready to lift the dog from the casket and exit the building. Her wails soon prompted my supervisor to enter the room, and it took us a long time to comfort her and assure her of the dog's death.

I recall this incident because never before had I seen someone in such immense sorrow and trauma. This woman was certainly dependent on her pet beyond normal boundaries. No human companion in her life cared at all that she grieved, or offered any support before or after the death of her pet. Her pain and isolation were so great that tears fill my eyes in remembrance. Eventually the woman sought professional therapy, which gradually brought her through her devastating loss and helped her begin to cope in many aspects of her life.

All of the mourning individuals I have counseled who suffered from total dependence on their pet—no matter what their religious practice, beliefs or personality—told me that they had contemplated suicide. I cannot overemphasize the importance of taking such threats seriously. People whose lives revolve around their pet believe that when their pet has died, life holds only despair and is no longer livable. If grieving friends or relatives tell you that they are considering suicide, believe them and help them to obtain proper therapy. In their own constructed reality, their pet may be a surrogate child, a mate for life or another such replacement human companion. Their pet may have been their only emotional support in life. Such individuals are the most self-destructive and must be properly treated by a professional therapist beyond the support they receive from you.

Clearly, our dependency on our pets has drastically changed since early eras of humanity. Today animals are rarely used to support our physical survival, whether hunting for food or herding the family's flock of sheep. Now their roles are psychological—as emotional stabilizers and family support. Our pets reflect our self-image and our ego-strength as individuals.

Elders and Pets

Our elders are shamefully mistreated and neglected by our society. It is easy to realize why their love for a pet can be enormous and fulfilling. The elderly enjoy the human-pet bond in a special fashion, because their pets still depend on them and love them despite any physical problems they may experience as they age. This dependency renews their deteriorating sense of importance as people. As the five senses dwindle, depression may set in, and the savor of life can be lost. But even if the individual is ill or ignored by family, happiness can be restored by the presence of a loving animal companion.

The death of that beloved friend is a shock that feels like abandonment, especially if the individual has no close human companions. This can lead to depression and further ill health, and it is essential that family, doctors or social workers help the person to cope. This coping is often made easier by the fact that most elderly individuals have seen friends and family die, and have learned to become more philosophical than in their younger years.[4] This is not to say that their sorrow is less, but rather that it is more easily coped with and better aimed toward a positive, earlier resolution.

Sadly, our elders are talked to by family and medical staff as if they are children or mentally ill, and are often depicted in television commercials and advertisements as senseless, mindless "old fools." Our elders want to regain the joy of life and once more be considered worthwhile. Caring for a pet can revitalize an elderly person's life and his or her identity as an individual capable of being appreciated, cherished and loved. When there is no one to fulfill an elderly person's life, an animal companion is the best medicine.

Pet Bereavement Awareness of Society

Our grief over our departed pets and its psychological consequences have generated a new social phenomenon in our Western culture. In the hope of extending the lives of our animal friends, we often we take better care of them than of ourselves. With so many individuals devoted to their animal companions, pet death care has become more practiced, recognized and profitable for industry. The evolution of extensive pet-related industries has prompted new recognition and awareness by medical professionals and the like of this once ignored human-animal bond.

Grieving pet guardians have asked me frequently, "Please tell me the truth—is it really all right for me to mourn my pet so much? My friends and family tell me my pet was just an animal and I'm foolish to put myself through such distress." Indeed, many people still feel that such grief is a ridiculous, self-produced, self-deceiving trauma. Unless your human companions in life are "animal people," it is likely they will dismiss your sorrow and criticize you. Rest assured that mourning your pet is indeed normal and should be recognized and dealt with in a healthy manner. Ignorant individuals who attack you at this most vulnerable time are simply demonstrating their psychological inadequacy.[5]

Criticism and ignorance of pet mourning is waning as our society recognizes and accepts our grief, and offers the assistance of mental health professionals. Nonetheless, be prepared to find that at least one person will discount your grief and determine that you are acting inappropriately. Remember that not everyone feels as you do concerning the human-animal bond, or has experienced the gratification and personal happiness of loving a pet.

When my cat Lester was tragically hit by a car, my neighbor called me at work and informed me, sobbing. I was shocked and devastated, and literally could not function enough even to respond. After a moment of silence, all I could say was, "Thank you. I cannot tell you how much I appreciate your letting me know. I'll take care of it." I was in an artificial state of calm that may have come from temporary disbelief. Soon, I was sobbing and so hysterical that my boss thought my parent or husband, or at least a human loved one, had died. When he found out that it was my cat, he was annoyed. When I couldn't proceed with my work and an hour later requested to take half a personal day, he refused. Instead of being able to go home and remove my cat's corpse from the road and make necessary arrangements for her body, I had to stay at work, where I could not mentally or physically function.

My sympathetic co-workers told me they would finish my projects for the day. I telephoned my town Animal Control officer and spoke with a very nasty gentleman who refused to pick up Lester's body. I was infuriated; after all, it was his job to remove animal carcasses from the roads in my town. Attempting to remain calm, I resorted to pleading and asked that he simply put her body in a bag and leave her on the front porch of my home. Finally, he agreed. Next, I called my husband at work and asked if on his lunch break he could take Lester's body to a pet crematorium to place on hold until I could make arrangements for her cremation.

Depending on your personality, you might have handled the situation differently. I know individuals who have walked out and quit their jobs under such circumstances. When you are overwhelmed by grief and need a day or two away from work to make suitable arrangements and calm down, I recommend simply telling your employer that there has been a death in your immediate family. This is the truth. If your employer were to know that the departed one was your pet, he or she might not be so compassionate. Don't provide details or excuses. If asked who died, simply state that you are too upset to talk about it. You do not have to reveal any facts. Be assertive, but not confrontational. If you are denied the time off, at least you tried. More than likely your employer will grant you a day or two.

Another lesson that can be drawn from the story of Lester's death is that it is best to consider ahead of time what arrangements you will make if anything should happen to your pet. Preparing now will make it easier later to make the final arrangements and grieve for your pet. There is nothing wrong with pre-planning your pet's burial or cremation, or considering how you might best deal with the loss. We will talk more about such plans in later chapters.

Our unique bond with our pets is a treasured part of our lives forever. When our pet dies, a part of us dies as well; we miss their participation in our inner selves, personal thoughts and true feelings, and we have lost the enchantment they bring to our lives. That part of us can be reclaimed, however, through the relationships we can experience with other pets and people. But the mourning may take much time to work through, and at first even one's religious beliefs, such as the concept of reincarnation or the belief in uniting again with our beloved pets in Summerland, or heaven, are not enough to ease our emotional pain.

An End of an Era in Life

The death of your pet marks the end of an era in your life. Even once the phases of mourning are identified and resolved, the aftershocks will continue far beyond the conclusion of the mourning period. It is normal to relive grief that was suffered years ago, or to have occasional sadness. I lost a rabbit some years ago who died of a digestive problem of which I had been unaware. I mourned him for nearly three weeks and battered myself with guilt. A neighbor who had used to raise rabbits assured me that rabbits are fragile creatures, and that my rabbit's health disorder was common and difficult to detect. It was her kind explanation and education that enabled me to stop torturing myself.

Although I resolved my tremendous grief, just the other day I walked into a farm and feed store and came across a tub full of baby rabbits. I remembered my rabbit with sorrow, yet smiled in tearful joy recalling how he had played with my dog Sasha, loved to burrow in my houseplant soil and had an unusual fascination with my vacuum cleaner. To this day I can see him sweetly nudge me with his chin for attention.

I sympathize with the seemingly endless agony of heart, soul and body that you feel at the loss of your pet. It does not seem fair that such wonderful, innocent and loving creatures should have such short life spans compared to our own. But for as long as we live, we will have all of our special pets with us when we chuckle in remembering their silly ways, or smile at the thought of their greeting us when we come home.

Death can be seen as a gracious relief for a sick pet, or as a tragic, untimely unfairness. The first, however, is not any easier to

cope with than the last. The grieving pet guardian embarks on a
lonely, emotional walk down the path of grief, but that path will
lead to the realm of resolution.

2

The Bereavement Process

IN THIS CHAPTER, WE WILL DISCUSS THE MANY VARIETIES OF GRIEF, and all the emotions you may experience in your bereavement. You will learn how to meet each emotion courageously and aim toward resolution. Much of the information within this chapter can benefit you in the tragic loss of a human relative, friend or companion as well. It is often said that the grieving process for a departed pet is similar to that for a beloved human. Many people are insulted by this comparison, but as we examine each phase of mourning you'll come to understand why it has been made.

What Is Death?

Before we can begin to understand the emotional components of pet bereavement, we need to discuss the greatest mystery of life—death.

Since the living cannot have definite knowledge of what death is, we tend to feel uncomfortable about death and avoid talking about it. Most people fear death, considering it an end to the existence of self. But, while we do not have definite knowledge of what death is, we should not automatically attribute negative traits to it. Death could be the most beautiful part of a creature's existence. Ancient scriptures and religious texts from around the world describe it as a divine, wonderful transition where physical pain and suffering are no more.

It is interesting to note that ancient civilizations existing today regard death very differently than we are accustomed to doing. The people of ancient cultures are not fooled by false claims that human beings can control nature or rewrite natural law. To them, death is not a mistake or accident but a natural part of life, just as birth is.

Along these lines, some modern religious thought teaches that death is not to be feared, but must be accepted as part of a natural cycle whose rules govern all existence. From the moment of birth, life is understood as a journey leading to death. From the moment you came into the material world as a physically incarnate human being, mortality was your own, as it is for every sentient being, with the promise and guarantee of death.

When was the beginning of you, me and every sentient creature? It was not the day of birth, because we existed in our mother's womb previous to that day. Does each sentient being begin existence at the moment of conception? Though we take on a physical form at conception, I believe that our unique, true selves existed before that time, and live through many different physical incarnations as we travel the path toward enlightenment.

Many religions teach that the soul—ageless and non-physical, and containing the essence of the Creator—travels through life, death and a form of rebirth. In this cycle of rebirth, death is a creative process whereby the soul is returned to its origin for renewal and revitalization. Operating not as an enemy but as an advisor of change, death prompts transition from one state of being to another. Just as every little change in life can be considered a kind of death and rebirth, life and death can be compared to transitions we have observed on a smaller scale. We might think of life as our waking time, and death as sleep time, when we do not cease to exist but temporarily withdraw from the waking experience.

In this whole context of the continuity of life, the law of karma operates. In certain Eastern religions, it is believed that the race, sex, place of birth and other factors of a lifetime are determined by the soul's actions—and lessons learned—in a past life. This phenomenon, known as karma, guides the soul in its development. It is a tool and a law of action: if you commit negative action in this lifetime, negative action will be returned to you in another lifetime. If you act positively in this lifetime, then positive action will be granted to you in another incarnation. The lives that we live today determine the degree of perfection of the soul at physical death and subsequent rebirth.

Each rebirth, based upon the triumphs and failures of former lifetimes, is an opportunity for you to reach your potential and develop your self. If your physical body ceases to function and dies before enlightenment, your soul must then return to earth in another physical body and continue the process of learning, seeking and striving for the ultimate goal of enlightenment. When after many rebirths perfection is obtained, the cycle is completed and the soul returns to the divine source from which it originated.

Hence, life force continues after death—but the exact form it takes is unknown. Many people believe that when the body dies the soul travels to a non-physical reality, sometimes called "heaven." Some people believe that in heaven there are no forms, only beings that exist in oneness with the supreme energy of all life. Others consider heaven a land of endless summer, where animals, people, plants—all sentient life—coexist. Some religions believe that the soul surveys the past life after death. Lessons achieved or failed are reviewed, and when the time is right, the soul returns to earth and life begins once more.

Some believe that a personality, or ego-form, may remain constant from one life to the next, with the ability to access past lives through the memory; this phenomenon is called *reincarnation*. Others may look forward to *resurrection*, the best-known belief of both ancient Egyptian and Christian religions. The ancient Egyptians believed that at the end of physical life, the astral body would function only if the physical body remained uncorrupted; the early Christians believed that the physical body would live again.

Whether you believe in reincarnation or resurrection in the spiritual world, there is no question that your pet will make the journey to the afterlife and will eternally maintain your loving bond in the spiritual realm. Since all living creatures contain life force, are born, and physically die, it makes sense that animals have souls. All living creatures need air, water, food, warmth and more. We are all a part of the same universe, and the Wheel of Life affects us all. All sentient beings may experience the process of soul enlightenment and perfection sought in incarnation.

We can experience some kinds of rebirth in the course of a single lifetime. Carl Jung wrote of a phenomenon called *initiation*, which is a time for *renovatio*, or renewal. It is a partial rebirth in that the nature of the personality, or ego-form, is not changed, but evolves in a new direction. Weak parts are strengthened, healed and improved. The final initiation is a process of transmutation, a complete rebirth in that the essence of personality is changed. *Indirect transformation* refers to rebirth experienced through participation in mystery rites, such as seasonal rituals celebrating the transformation of nature and the inner transformation process of self. Through meditation and ritual, through healing and personal growth, we may be able to achieve our own transformation in response to the natural transition of our beloved pet.

The Grieving Process

The grieving process can last anywhere from a couple of days or several weeks to many months. Exactly how long you will grieve cannot and should not be measured or predicted. Each individual will react differently, and there is no generic estimate to apply. There is no right or wrong time frame for mourning. People feel tremendous internal conflict and emotional pain during the grieving process. Often additional stress is caused by a lack of human support and understanding of the grief that accompanies pet loss. No matter the length of grieving, everyone should be allowed all the time and support they need to see them through the hardship.

A woman called me one afternoon, distraught, and said, "My cat Bobbi died two days ago and yet I no longer feel affected by it. Is this normal? Shouldn't I still be mourning? I loved him so much, yet the sorrow has been lifted so soon. I feel guilty that I have gotten over him so quickly."

Depending upon an individual's spiritual beliefs, pre-planned arrangements, the cause of the pet's death or loss and many other factors, a response such as this can be normal. The death was not sudden or unexpected; Bobbi had died of cancer, which the woman had known would probably kill him within that year or the next. This knowledge helped her prepare emotionally for Bobbi's death. In addition, this woman had a strong spiritual faith and believed in reincarnation; she knew that she and her cat would reunite in the next life. She considered his death to be not an abrupt end but a transformation of their already existing relationship. Considering this, she was grieving normally. Unlike most pet guardians, she did not suffer separation anxiety, which prolongs the mourning, because her beliefs did not allow for it. Though she was hysterical for two days, her strong beliefs carried her through the bereavement process quickly.

Those individuals who grieve for more than a few days or seem to be unable to cope for months are also normal mourners. Most of us, unlike Bobbi's guardian, will experience separation anxiety, which some psychologists regard as the key to the onset of the grieving process. The everyday normalcy of your life is suddenly lost along with your cherished pet. You are alone, in a state of shock, and your life feels empty and meaningless. Separation anxiety can be heightened by symbolic values you may have attached to your pet. The pet may have been cherished by a deceased friend, parent or lover, or may represent some special event in your life. Perhaps after an ugly divorce your pet was the only stable part of your life, and you have depended on your pet's affection. In such cases, your pet is a living symbol of an aspect of your life that is extremely important to you, and his or her death is a severe blow to your sense of security.

When these initial feelings escalate, other life stresses or underlying psychological issues can become overwhelming. It is my opinion that after a few weeks a great majority of the sorrow should be resolved, and that if depression is evident, or resolution has not occurred, one must seek help in the form of support groups or a therapist, because one may lack the resources that would enable one to cope with the loss.

While many people, fearful of death's power, wish to ignore or suppress the grieving process itself, denying your feelings can be emotionally harmful. The suppressed responses are real and devastating, and they must be released for healing to begin. When a loss is not sufficiently dealt with, then another calamity later in life may revive those repressed and unresolved feelings, adding old sorrow to new pain.[1]

Psychological Reactions

Our psychological reactions to the death of a beloved pet are meant to be recognized and dealt with, allowing healing to begin. Attempting to understand the phases of grief can help prepare you and guide you during the grieving process. The way we deal with these phases generally determines how long mourning will prevail.

Each mourning is personal. Because of our individual fears, religious beliefs, personality traits and other internal factors, each individual will grieve differently.

The phases of the grieving process do not necessarily appear in a specific order and then disappear. Depending on your situation and personality, all the phases of grieving[2]—shock, disbelief, denial, anger, solitude, guilt, depression and resolution—can appear in a different order than described in this text or may surface simultaneously.

The intense emotional stress you suffer during your mourning can cause you to question your sanity. You should not worry about your sanity as long as you are coping. There will be temporary agony, but healthy coping will allow it to wane. Only when post-traumatic stress syndrome, depression, thoughts of suicide, denial or other destructive emotions surface and remain is professional help necessary.

Nevertheless, there are some abnormal behavior patterns that can signal danger and should be mentioned here. Overreaction is often characterized by fatigue, intensified irritability, sleeplessness, extreme withdrawal, excessive anger, antisocial behavior, persistent nightmares and hallucinations of hearing or seeing the deceased pet.[3] I am not referring to the summoning of your pet in meditation, ritual or welcome spiritual contact, but to the uninvited and hazardous symptoms of a mind nearing mental breakdown.

When I was a little girl, my family suffered the tragic loss of our Labrador retriever, Sally. Sally was in her elder years, and one night when my mother let her outside to "do her business" she just lost her way in the darkness. My mother called to her and searched for her, but Sally had wandered onto a nearby road, and had been hit by a car. I remember the driver, a neighbor woman, coming to our house crying with the news. The woman was near hysteria, and we had to console her as well as deal with our initial shock.

I was not allowed to go with my parents to the accident scene. When Sally came home with them from the veterinarian's, she was bandaged and severely injured. The veterinarian had said that if she did not eat, drink or appear strong in a day or two he strongly recommended euthanasia (putting Sally to death by injection, in this case). Sally did not improve, and my family agonized at watching her suffer. She was put to sleep two days later.

For days and weeks after Sally's death I sensed her presence. At night I heard Sally's claws clicking across the kitchen floor, as if she were walking about the house. On two of these occasions I got out of bed in the middle of the night, feeling a spark of hope that she was indeed risen from the dead or somehow home alive. I thought I saw Sally on many occasions—rounding the corner from the kitchen into the living room, sitting in a corner or walking outside in our yard. This was very frightening for me as a child.

This type of response to pet loss indicates post-traumatic stress syndrome and should not be ignored if it occurs frequently enough to disrupt the sufferer's life. My experiences eventually stopped, but many psychologists and medical professionals believe that until such symptoms are adequately dealt with, they can only be suppressed. Without the intervention of a professional psychologist, post-traumatic stress syndrome can fester and create problems in an individual's life. In order to release these psychological disturbances, professional help is necessary.

Not everyone suffers from post-traumatic stress syndrome when a loved one dies. Often, those who do are already emotionally injured or dealing with enormous stress in their lives. The impact of another trauma may simply be too overwhelming for the individual to cope with alone.

Grief is not a sign of neurosis, a mental disorder, or an act of extreme behavior. Mourning the loss of loved ones is natural and a completely healthy process, so long as one is not so distraught that one harms oneself or others. The mourner needs guidance, understanding, support, caring, and someone compassionate to speak with about his or her feelings.

Phases of Mourning
Initial Shock and Disbelief
Quite often the discovery of your pet's death will cause some degree of shock, even in individuals who knew their pet was dying of an illness or injury. Inability to function physically or think clearly are sometimes the first signs of an emotional overload. Powerful and overwhelming psychological reactions trip your thought processes and stun your mind. There may be a feeling of numbness in mind and body, or a sense of inability to physically react at all. Some individuals repeatedly ask in disbelief if their pet is truly dead, despite very specific proof. This is a sign that they have not accepted reality.

This inability to accept or believe in the death of your pet is caused by a powerful but temporary defense of the mind. After receiving any unbearable input, the mind goes into shock to protect itself from a sudden onslaught of powerful emotions. It is nature's last defense, shielding us from violence that can be done to the mind by unbearable stimuli.[4]

The mind's defenses are so powerful that you may seem hypnotized and unable to accept input that supports the overwhelming news. It has been proven that some types of amnesia are caused by overwhelming shock and disbelief.[5] We know that some people have survived a violent or extremely emotional trauma by totally blocking out the memory of it. These memories may surface suddenly and uncontrollably years later, or the individual may never recall what happened. No matter the defense maneuver, your mind is stalling in coping with circumstances that are unbearable.

Your temporary shock and disbelief will wear off and give way to other intense emotional reactions. Usually more than one emotion surfaces at once, further distorting your view of the situation. Patience and time will lead to healing; meanwhile, these emotional responses are necessary in order to cope with tragedy. You will feel helpless, violated and dismayed for quite some time before you're able to cope with your loss.

When I recall the death of my beloved cat Lester, I can clearly identify my brief period of shock and disbelief, which I would say lasted almost four hours. I soon became capable of accepting her death, especially when my husband, Phil, called me at work to say that he had taken her body to the pet crematorium. I knew at that moment that there was no possible error—Phil had seen her body, and knew it was our Lester. The shock waned, as did the awful guilt, but then anger and other emotions evolved.

Denial

Denial typically develops after the initial shock and disbelief (though sometimes other emotional responses, such as guilt or anger, will precede it). It is one of the earliest phases of grieving and is often confused initially with the disbelief that accompanies the shock of learning about the death. Denial, however, involves a deliberate and total rejection of reality. The individual may acknowledge that the death has happened, but consciously attempts to refute it.

The devastating finality of death causes some individuals to approach it as a bad dream or somehow unreal. The passionate desire to believe that the pet is still alive and all will soon be well again is a stumbling block in the grief process that will recede in time. It is normal to experience a brief period of denial that resolves quickly.

Denial is justifiable and valuable when it serves as a temporary protection from overwhelming problems. The mind practices such defense mechanisms whenever reality offers too much pain too quickly and we need a time-out. Immediate and full acceptance at the time of a loved one's death is nearly impossible for anyone. Each individual will experience denial differently, and tolerance and patience are crucial during the hardship of making the transition.

Denial becomes abnormal when an individual is convinced that some action can be performed to bring back the lost life. I do not refer here to the belief in a life after death. Considering your pet spiritually alive and ascending toward divinity for reincarnation, transmutation or resurrection, and believing that communication with your pet is possible, does not indicate denial of the fact that your pet has crossed the threshold from physical existence into the realm of death. Performing rituals to aid in your healing, or acts of communication between you and your deceased pet, are healthy ways of coping. I refer instead to cases in which the bereaved person strives to locate the "missing" pet, convinced that the pet's physical disappearance has been caused by something other than death. The individual may even believe that the "disappearance" of the pet was caused by the attending veterinarian or by some conspiracy. When a person denies the reality of a pet's death despite having personally witnessed the evidence of his or her death, professional help is necessary.

I have witnessed this phenomenon firsthand as a pet bereavement counselor. One woman I counseled could not accept the physical death of her dog. She telephoned me frequently to discuss her anger and resentment toward her lawyer, her veterinarian and her family, because they refused to help her uncover the conspiracy behind her dog's sudden disappearance. Knowing that her dog was indeed deceased and on hold in the pet cemetery's freezer, I attempted to gently coax her into the realization that her dog had died of natural causes as found in the autopsy. I explained that I had handled her dog personally since his arrival at the facility. The more I tried to assure her, the angrier and more resistant she became. I recommended professional intervention to her husband, who later informed me that she had refused. He wept for his wife. Her entire life was dedicated to unveiling a conspiracy that did not exist. She was no longer mentally living in our reality, it seemed.

On the day of her dog's wake and burial, the woman began to accept what had happened. Perhaps actually seeing and touching her beloved dog, and witnessing his burial process, provided the evidence her mind required. In some cases, burial or cremation arrangements act as a ritual for self-transformation, and physical and emotional participation in the ritual offers the first step toward healing. Considering that this woman had refused professional therapy, she and her family were very fortunate that the wake and burial were enough to finally bring her through denial.

Initial denial is a protective exercise that allows us to live in painless limbo for a short time. Before long, the realities of our lives intervene, forcing the fact of death and the need to cope back to our attention and allowing us to proceed through the developmental phases of the grieving-healing process. However, studies of human psychology have discovered two types of denial that can arise after initial denial: bargaining denial and fantasy denial.

Often the immediate responsibilities, such as the care of the pet's body, have been performed when bargaining denial begins. Usually you are alone and smothered in grief, feeling helpless and frustrated. You sense your pet's presence still in your home and anticipate the familiar sight of him or her napping by a favorite chair or playing in his or her cage. There is a void in your home, a feeling that the home environment is no longer real—as if you are experiencing a time warp of some sort, or a temporary loss of reality.

In your confusion, you begin to consider that perhaps your pet isn't really deceased and life may revert to the way it was. When these hopes start to dwindle, the bargaining begins. Perhaps you bargain with your deity, whispering "I'll be a better person" or other messages to the gods, hoping to trade future good behavior for the renewed life of your pet. If your pet's death is expected, as in the case of terminal illness, this denial might play an impassioned role before the actual death. But it never works, and the fact of death still remains.

Fantasy denial resembles a child-like state of pretending. You may fill your pet's water and food dishes or toss his or her toys upon the floor with the notion that somehow your pet will come running from beyond to play and be with you again. These fantasies are beautiful displays of love, but you need to remember that they are not real, that you must accept your pet's death and learn to cope. Your pet has died, time moves you onward through life, and whether you put effort into resolution or not, you will go on.

These two types of denial are typical if you did not witness the death of your pet. You might have heard of the death from a neighbor or family member, or, in a gesture of love, the witnesses quickly disposed of your pet's body, hoping to shield you from pain. Although the gesture is kind and meant to be helpful, in the long run it may cause you to have difficulty in immediately accepting the reality. "Where is the body?" you may plead. "Did you actually see what happened? Maybe it wasn't my pet—may it was someone else's that you thought was mine." When a stranger is the messenger, it can seem appalling that an outsider to such a private, loving relationship should inform you of something so intensely personal.

Many veterinarians have become educated and sensitive (through experience and common sense) to the denial stage of grieving. Veterinarian teaching hospitals train students in handling the pet guardian's grief and initial emotional responses, and one of the most important principles is that the pet guardian should view the pet's body if possible, and receive the utmost assistance in making arrangements for the body, along with emotional support.

Your veterinarian, if truly an animal lover and care provider, will be your closest ally in the battle of resolution. The veterinarian usually views the body of your pet and has a role in your plans for burial, cremation and other arrangements. The loving veterinarian will know that the first stage of grieving should be conducted in privacy, somewhere in the clinic or hospital, between you and your deceased pet.

Though the veterinary staff means well, grieving pet guardians often avoid emotional support when it is offered. As the technician attempts to console, the pet guardian may stand rigid, presenting a calm, strong and emotionally collected persona. Anyone who has worked with people and animals through a pet death knows that this behavior comes from fear—fear of one's own responses, of the finality of death and of the impending self-confrontation.

Because we as human beings are trained to avoid acknowledging the ultimate reality of death, we are especially prone to denial. We understand that death comes to all living things, and yet our human society teaches that talking and thinking about death are somehow taboo. Fearful and mystified in contemplating what death must be like, and feeling that it has no place in our living and loving world, most people prefer not to think about death at all.

It is difficult for us to accept that death is a part of life and that, like the changing seasons of nature, it is inevitable and cannot be rationally denied. Yet we realize that as each day passes, all life grows closer to the threshold of death. Death awaits all living creatures. The sudden death of a loved one may cause a temporary sense that the ascent to the spiritual world is untimely and unjustified, but we come to understand that the transition from physical existence to the spiritual world is one of growth, evolution and promising rebirth—in the form of reincarnation, resurrection, or living a spiritual existence in the presence of God. You need to not deny your pet's experience of the glorious transition into the realm of your deity. Your pet has moved beyond physical existence and further evolves in spiritual existence. Denying that physical death has occurred will only cause misery for you. Remember that your pet lives on in the spiritual world and is capable of communication with you. The transition of your pet's being is a cycle of his or her life, a new beginning and part of an inevitable cycle in your loving relationship.

In extreme cases of denial, the sufferer may feel pushed or criticized by other people, and other underlying concurrent psychological problems may become exacerbated. It is generally best to allow people to hold onto their denial until they are ready to let go on their own. The only exception is if there is a psychological risk, in which case the sufferer needs professional counseling or at least involvement with a support group. If the problem of denial is excessive and unyielding after about six weeks, it should be evaluated by a professional. If the individual is not willing, consult his or her family physician.

Anger

Being unable to understand or control death causes intense outrage for many people. Mourners' anger may prevent them from interacting with other people and fulfilling their responsibilities, which in turn causes frustration. The anger is usually released at random, supported by self-created excuses as to why venting such rage at other people is appropriate.

Anger can be projected outward or dealt with internally. It arrives in many forms and is handled in many ways. In circumstances where guilt or self-blame prevails, there is often an irrational assignment of responsibility and displaced blame to other individuals besides oneself.

The total helplessness you may feel at the death of your human or animal loved one is frustrating, and your anger must be dealt with in a healthy fashion. More often than not, anger is incorrectly dealt with because of our lack of expertise in using and resolving anger appropriately. It seems as if your pet has been snatched from your loving embrace and your special relationship has been severed. When we are immersed in the passionate sorrow of bereavement, anger is much more difficult to handle and resolve than in many other circumstances.

For a time, you may feel anger toward your God or Goddess. Though you may believe in reincarnation, transmutation or resurrection, you may still feel angry when you wonder why your pet had to die *now*. Though you understand that your pet is still united with you through the spirit, it is normal for you to feel angered at the loss of his or her physical life. Many people feel that a deceased pet has been "taken," and wish to blame someone or something for what seems to be an untimely or violent loss. Their sense of proportion can be distorted by frustration and rage; regardless of religious ideology, sometimes this distortion is impossible to avoid. Loss of perspective seems unavoidable at this stage of the mourning process, and situations that normally would be considered trivial or meaningless take on an exaggerated importance.

Keep in mind that although anger is termed "irrational" in a psychological analysis of loss due to death, we are human beings, emotional creatures, who live longer lives than many of our beloved animal neighbors on earth. When we do not fully understand something that has happened to us, we feel confused and bewildered, and usually this leads to anger. Some anger is to be expected, and you should not feel guilty or unworthy if you experience it.

Any God, Goddess or person within our lives can be made into a scapegoat for our anger at this trying time. Often the veterinarian and hospital staff involved in a pet's health care and death arrangements are the first and easiest targets for anger and blame. Deep within, we know these people are acting appropriately in attempting to help our animal companions and have their best interests at heart, yet our helplessness and search for answers may cause us to blame them wrongfully.

During this stage of mourning, it is also common to internalize anger. You may blame yourself for a variety of weaknesses or faults, or for decisions that failed to prevent your pet's death or sustain a dying life. But self-destructiveness is the only outcome of the potent force of withheld anger. If you are forewarned and prepared for such a response, you can limit its negative effects.

When we feel confused or helpless, meditation and ritual can unfold our minds to new realization. In meditation we can bring anger forward, examine the emotion from many angles and diffuse it through understanding and knowledge within the higher self. Reaching toward the higher self is a great act of self-help that can replace self-defeatism with regained control and perspective. Healing coupled with guidance sought of the God or Goddess can uplift us from the struggles anger can create at such a time, when balance, understanding and overcoming negative emotion is so crucial.

Keeping anger submerged is not the answer. You deserve much better in mourning. Your higher self, your faith and the guidance of your deity are tools that can assist you in letting go of anger. The exercise below can bring about a healthy release of anger by making the emotion surface into an objective state. This exercise should be done for a few days. It is not a test, but an intensely personal, subjective process. Attempting to finish it in one sitting will result in further frustration and impatience.

This exercise can be conducted during a quiet moment of privacy. You need a pencil or pen, a sheet of paper, and the intention of being totally honest with yourself. The best resource that can help you through this difficult moment is yourself, and the ability to use that resource depends upon the utmost truth from within.

Anger Assessment Exercise

Difficult as it may be, try to clear your mind of the overwhelming emotions of your loss. Meditation can help you clear your thoughts and focus. Your goal is to recognize the anger that you are experiencing and strive toward resolution.

Take time as needed to maintain as calm a state of being as possible. Once ready, take your pencil or pen and begin your assessment by heading the sheet of paper with the subject, "ANGER." Then:

- Numbering each response and skipping one line between each, list the people you feel anger toward and why.
- List the names of individuals who have upset you in some way throughout your bereavement.
- After the names have been written, return to each one and write the ways each person has caused you additional distress.
- Next to this list, or on the back of the sheet of paper, write a list of places (such as the veterinary hospital or workplace), situations and any other individual or occurrence you feel has caused you additional stress during this time.
- After careful consideration and completion, place the list in storage and allow a few days to pass before examining it. This lapse of time will allow you greater objectivity.

When you resume the exercise, examine the list and consider, one by one, each named source that has caused you additional discomfort and pain.

People who have been insensitive and made hurtful comments regarding your mourning have caused you real pain, but consider what might be preventing them from understanding the loss you face. Might they have a problem facing death that causes them to adopt a callous attitude toward you? Because of your grief and anger, could you be making these individuals into additional problems for yourself? Are you ready to forgive those individuals who simply are not animal people and have no idea what it is like to have a loving relationship with animals? Can you forgive those people who simply cannot relate, or understand, or who say inappropriate things to you?

In the case of your anger toward your veterinarian or hospital staff, could it be that they tried to sustain your pet's life to the best of their ability and cannot be held accountable for what was destined to be? Could your anger at your animal care providers possibly be due to your emotional turmoil at needing someone or something to blame?

When we hurt the most we will inflict our rage and pain upon those people who truly matter in our lives and who, it is felt, somehow failed to help us when we needed their support. Often when we sit crying and hurting, desperate for love and understanding, some people simply cannot provide the help we expect or desire. Some individuals simply have their own fears of death that make it uncomfortable for them to comment on your loss. Others may not know what to say to make you feel better. It is not that they do not understand, sympathize or care; in most cases, they are probably afraid that discussing death will upset you further. It is also possible in your grief to misinterpret someone's words. For example, when a pet dies of terminal illness, a loved one might say, "Fluffy is better off now. You should be grateful that she died when she did." But you may hear, "What happened to Fluffy isn't important—you shouldn't cry about it." Recognize the difference between what was actually meant and what you may have heard as a result of your mourning.

Trying to learn more about yourself and your anger through objective thinking will help to ease your pain. When you are honest and frank with yourself, you may realize that there is no logical reason for you to be angry at others. Perhaps you are really angry at yourself. Or there may be a real reason for your anger, and you are unwilling to recognize it and deal with it appropriately.

When anger evolves within us, it is difficult to think clearly, and easy to jump to conclusions or overreact. At times our frustration, disappointment and emotional pain keep us from noticing and accepting other people's human frailty and personal problems. If a loved one or friend states that you are overreacting in anger, it may hurt your feelings, but it may be true. It is important to discover what else may be subconsciously upsetting you, and resolve it.

Anger does have legitimate uses, but it can easily become abusive. Consider whether it is really helpful to be angry at death, at reality—or at yourself for being unable to defeat death or to fully understand it. Recognize that you will not be able to memorialize your pet in a positive manner if you are troubled by anger. Understand that this is a phase of mourning that will disappear if you allow yourself the time to cope, have patience with others and permit it to pass.

Solitude

We have seen how people who seem judgmental about your grief can catch you off balance at this deeply emotional time. You may be told that mourning your pet is overreacting. "It was just a pet," someone may tell you, "so get another. It'll make you feel better," or, "Why are you so upset about a pet? It's just an animal, not a person." You may wonder how people can make such cruel comments when they don't fully understand the circumstances that led to your pet's death, or the special, close relationship you had with your pet. From their limited perspective, these people may consider that they are making a legitimate point, but as long as they cannot accept your bereavement for your pet, they will fail to satisfy your needs and expectations at this trying time.

When your emotional strength has plummeted, and your feelings of guilt and sorrow arise, you are often unprepared to handle such commentary constructively. Criticism from others activates your defense mechanism of anger, which in turn may cause you to seek solitude. Solitude is not the same as the withdrawal associated with depression, which we will discuss later. Solitude is a safe haven we create to avoid the presence of others. In grieving, we may choose solitude in order to guard against inflicting our pain upon unsuspecting victims or exposing ourselves to the ridicule of ignorant individuals. Mourners often seek solitude because they do not know how to react to those around them in their confusion, sorrow and perhaps resentment. You may tell yourself that your co-workers, family, friends, and even your spirituality cannot help you, and that it is not worth seeking comfort in them. You may find yourself drowning in suffering, misinterpreting the responses of others and producing unexplained barriers, fending off any outside assistance.

At this vulnerable time, you are seeking an outlet for your powerful, brewing emotions. You are psychologically imbalanced by grief and trying to cope; everyday situations and decisions are suddenly difficult or emotionally charged. Keep in mind that even the relationships that are strained by someone who cannot help you at this needy time have positive value and significance. If you allow yourself to be hurt by that person's lack of understanding or compassion, you defeat yourself. If you punish him or her with angry words or permanent alienation, you may regret it later.

Remember, there are other human beings out there who consider pets as mere childish playthings, a waste of time and money, or possessions—like any other piece of property.

Remember, too, that death is a frightening and threatening subject for many people. People in your life may not feel able to discuss it with you. Despite your breaking heart and your need for their support, you cannot push or demand consoling. Your loved ones are human, too, and may be incapable of helping you cope due to their own fright and uncertainty.

There is nothing wrong with taking solitary time to reflect on your relationship with your pet, and to mourn. However, seeking solitude in avoidance of people who you feel may criticize you is not healthy. Instead, you need to be able to positively respond to such situations.

There are three typical responses to a perceived assault upon your grief:

- Reacting with anger and bitterness
- Being caught off-guard in such a manner that you don't know what to say. In your embarrassment or confusion, you say nothing, giving the impression that you agree with the offensive statement. This response may occur in an interaction with someone in authority—perhaps a boss or supervisor at your workplace.
- Preparing and planning in advance

When an insensitive person strikes, you can use a planned response, such as: "It seems to me that you are not an animal person and have probably never experienced the special bond you can have with a pet. You don't understand how much I miss the love and companionship my pet brought to my life. Please don't be so quick to judge me, as I feel deep, personal feelings of loss at this time."

You can say something to that effect, in a calm but firm tone of voice. You do not want to seem offensive or defensive. You want to exhibit non-threatening responses that still make your feelings clear. You will enlighten other people who may not understand the intensity of your grief, and you will also protect yourself from the further emotional upset of a charged confrontation—and perhaps even save a valuable relationship.

Keep in mind that this person has no clue what it is like to feel as you do, or he or she wouldn't have been so insensitive.

It is important to remain calm and tolerant when dealing with such people, especially in a work environment. Bursting into a defensive rage will only cause your superiors to question your ability to handle your job through this and future crises.

Passionate, unconsidered reactions do not "straighten out" the rude or insensitive individuals, but cause delay in your healing and your ability to cope in your life without your pet. Rather than hiding from the world for fear of criticism or ridicule, practice communicating effectively and concentrate on those people who are sensitive to your loss.

Guilt

In intense bereavement, you may feel that you somehow failed in obligation to your pet. You may accuse yourself of personal inadequacy, feeling that you have failed to perform as well as you could have. Sometimes people actually feel that this perceived inadequacy caused their pet to die.

Guilt is a psychological construct based on insecurity or a negative self-evaluation, and is a normal response to failing some duty or obligation.[6] It is not the same as disappointment, but is related to shame, and is associated with failing at a level well within our competence. Scientific research and professional analysis conclude that guilt is a human emotion and is not observed in wildlife. However, in training and scolding our pets for violating an expected or proper behavior, we've discovered the capacity for guilt in domesticated animals. A scolded dog will lie down some feet away from us, regarding us with saddened eyes, and eventually will approach and nudge us in apology. This demonstrates that pets can feel guilty of inappropriate behavior even several minutes after the incident.

In caring for an animal, you accept responsibility for all aspects of his or her life. You are completely responsible for your pet's nutrition, medical attention, quality of life, sexual status, playmates, whereabouts and more. Your pet becomes dependent upon you and you become emotionally dependent upon him or her. It is one of the purest "give and take" relationship forms. When your customary duties toward your pet cease to exist at his or her death, you may become victim to your own mind, which creates a sense of guilt derived from the loss of responsibility and haunts you with the thought that those responsibilities were not carried out properly.

Often, we are not able to control the circumstances in which our pet dies or is lost. When we have not been able to protect him or her, we come to believe we must have been able to do something, but failed. "If I had taken Penny out for her morning walk at the usual time, she would not have seen the cat, chased it into the road and been killed! How could I have let this happen?" Our pets' dependence often places us in a godlike role in their lives. Remember to recognize that you are still fallible, that despite your loving efforts you are not capable of controlling fate and the random hazards of existence.

In many cases, the feeling of guilt arrives in the earliest stages of mourning, after disbelief and beside anger. So powerful are these emotions that they can distort all attempts at objective thinking. Your mind pours forth the products of fantasy: "I should have . . ." "I could have . . ." and "If only I had . . ." You begin to feel that your actions, or inactions, were insufficient. Humans strive for what we cannot reach and desire outcomes beyond our abilities and skill. We forget that we have no power over death.

Bereavement challenges whatever spiritual faith we may have. The newly bereaved yearn for answers, questioning their old beliefs. Sadly, no matter how we examine death, it will not make sense that an innocent, trusting, loving animal must die. But our mind, fearing to acknowledge that death is a fact of life we must learn to accept, produces feelings of guilt to give us the illusion of control. By focusing on the physical plane, where we have some power over events, we subconsciously attempt to assert control over an unfathomable mystery.

When my cat Louis died after being hit by a car, I kneeled upon the earth before his home burial site, sobbing. Tormented by anger and guilt, I demanded a reassuring answer, once and for all, from the Gods: What was death? Would I ever see Louis again? Was he now transformed and existing in another realm unknown to me? Was he just gone—his existence swallowed up in time like a black hole? I couldn't seem to connect with my earlier spiritual beliefs about death.

I mentally battered myself with accusations of irresponsibility. I asked myself how I could have allowed him to be an indoor/outdoor cat when I knew the risks involved. How could I have been so negligent as to allow his outdoor activity when a highway was close by? The truth of the matter was that Louis had originally been an indoor cat, but after the day he snuck outside and got a taste of nature, he would throw "cat tantrums" if he wasn't allowed out when he wanted to go. (As cat guardians know, this means Louis knocked things off tables and literally climbed the walls.) He wanted to live exposed to nature, and in my opinion it was better that he enjoy five years of cat adventures and the pleasures of nature than live shut in the house against his desires.

Guilt is unfounded no matter what the circumstances. Dwelling on how we could have postponed, prevented or eased our pet's death only results in pain, not resolution. Such thinking is abusive and only punishes you when you are already in anguish. However, healthy self-analysis of what happened can aid in personal growth.

I resolved my anger, guilt and emotional pain over Louis's death by writing poems about my love for him, about what he meant to my life and what I was feeling as a result of his death. Writing these poems allowed me to release many buried emotions, uncover hidden personal problems that were adding to my distress, examine my irrational reactions and start my way toward resolution.

In certain individuals, perpetual guilt is a way of life; they think their self-punishment is well deserved for what or who they are. If you are such a person, you derive a negative emotional payoff from your guilt. This indicates that even before your loss you were already vulnerable and suffering in some way internally. There is no positive service in tormenting yourself; you only hurt yourself more with this guilt. Stop punishing yourself. You are a caring, loving individual who has suffered a deeply painful loss— give yourself compassion, not punishment. Console yourself as you would a human loved one in the same predicament. Take this time to give yourself tender loving care, and continue loving your pet, who, I assure you, has nothing but continuing love for you—not blame.

This may seem hard to believe, and your feelings of guilt may seem justified. But it may have been the time for your pet's death. And accidents do happen, despite our best intentions. Circumstances such as a cat escaping through an open door or window, a dog running into the road when left unattended for a second, or the pet who eats a poisonous plant are not uncommon. There are horrifying accounts of pet guardians accidentally causing the death of their own pet, such as a woman who threw out the garbage and later found that her kitten had hidden inside the garbage bag in play. Antifreeze claims many pet lives in the winter months, and pet guardians punish themselves with guilt. A pet may die during the application of anesthetic at the veterinary clinic, usually because of an underlying health problem, like a heart rhythm disorder, that went unnoticed. All of these examples seem preventable, but we must accept that we are fallible. We do our best to care for ourselves and our pets; that is all we can realistically do.

Wishing things had been different perpetuates negative energy within yourself. We are human beings, and we make mistakes. If we erred unintentionally, then don't we deserve compassion, forgiveness and release from the agony of guilt? When you accept the reality of your pet's death and continue living and loving, there is no more room for questioning yourself about what preventive measures you could have taken. Allow yourself to let go—show yourself compassion. This is a difficult task, and takes time and patience.

Sometimes people feel guilty at the thought that they will go to heaven, but their pets will not. Many religious denominations do not offer explanations, support or even discussion of an animal's role in human existence, much less where their souls travel at death.

When I was a child, my family attended an Episcopal church. One morning the Father mentioned in his sermon that animals, unfortunately, do not have souls. My father was clearly uncomfortable with that statement. After the sermon my father approached the clergyman and asked him if he thought animals went to heaven or had an afterlife. The Father answered, "No." My father responded that he did not need to go to heaven if there would be no animals, and our family never went back to that church.

I recall this story to make a point. Not all religions or people believe that animals have souls or experience an afterlife. But if you doubt either, I ask you this—do animals not breathe the air to live as we do? Are not their physical bodies and minds similar to our own, requiring air, water, food and survival instinct to live? In my thinking, humans are terribly arrogant to believe that only we have souls, that we are the only creatures of worth on this planet. As all living creatures have life-force, we all shall experience afterlife.

Do not feel guilty for believing that you and your pet will share the afterlife together if your religion states differently. It is not wrong for you to love your pet, even more than you love most people, and to desire to reunite in the afterlife. There is so little that science and religion truly understand about life, much less death. True belief is in your heart and soul—don't feel guilty about it.

Would your pet like to see you so saddened, guilty and unable to go on? If you had died, would you wish your pet to continue living a good, fulfilling life without you? Now is the time to call on the inner strength you'll need for resolution of your grief and direct your energy toward yourself. You can continue to be the wonderful person your pet so loved. Your duty now is to yourself, through constructive mourning, release from self-torment, cherishing the loving memories of your physical life with your pet and realizing that your pet's physical death has not ended your loving relationship.

Depression

During your mourning, it may seem that all that you can think or care about is your pet's death and your own terrible misery. Everything else in life seems unimportant. You feel numb, indifferent. You may feel a loss of internal strength. Each passing hour and day is deeply saddening. Your heart aches and you feel this may be a point of no return. This is depression.

Depression is usually the most difficult stage of your mourning. You may experience a wide range of symptoms: physical fatigue, listlessness, loss of ambition and desire, inability to concentrate, detachment from life, the need for solitude, discontentment and avoidance of normal daily activities, and upset of your normal sleep patterns. You may cry frequently and cease to find pleasure in the activities you used to enjoy, or in the company of loved ones. There is a void in your life, as if your sense of worth has slipped away. Psychic suffering and despair engulf you, and there seems to be no way to stop it.

Most everyone experiences depression at some time in life. For most people, it is a brief period of unrest, but for others it can be an intense emotional drowning. In bereavement, depression creeps upon you as an unconscious attempt to numb your pain and help you escape from suffering.

It is common for us to withdraw when situations in our lives become unbearable and our strong emotions make coping difficult. We may stop caring about what other people are doing or what is going on around us. In some respects, this can be helpful, because all of your energies need to be safely collected and focused toward resolution. But often, depression takes over our lives. Depression is so powerful that it suffocates even guilt. It removes the motivation to feel any emotion. No more shock, disbelief, denial, anger— there is only emptiness in your heart, soul and mind. Depression can become a roadblock on the path to recovery. In order to get through the grieving process, it must be overcome.

In this abyss of emptiness, caring friends who lend support and try to help you may be perceived as invasive and harassing. Their efforts annoy you, because you want to be left alone to mourn. You may even feel that the loss of your pet is too personal and intense to share with the people closest to you. You may wonder how another person could possibly understand your sadness, and construct a barrier of self-protection from outside influence. Your sorrow for your pet and the emptiness within yourself stand between you and the rest of the world. You tell yourself that nothing matters anymore, and that no one in the entire world could understand what you are going through, or truly care.

The fear and resentment you feel when your spiritual or philosophical beliefs cannot give you answers about death, about where your pet has gone at death or if you will see him or her again, only add to your hopelessness and grief. There seems to be no value to life when the answers you need cannot be found.

In your sadness, consider that nature provides the answers you seek. In the many pet losses I have experienced, I too have looked for these answers, and developed a personal philosophy. Whether you enjoy gardening or not, visualize for a moment that you are kneeling on the earth, next to a hole in fertile soil, and that in your cupped hands you hold a lily bulb. Visualize yourself gently placing the bulb into the hole and filling in the hole with fertile soil. Let your tears of grief fall upon the newly planted soil. See the first sprout of life grow upward from the soil. At an awesome rate, it grows to full form, with the most beautiful vibrant orange blossom you have ever seen. Take a moment to witness its life and beauty. Then, visualize the lily petals falling from the stem one by one, until all have fallen, the lily withers and dies, and nothing is left but bare soil. Dig into the soil with your hands and remove the bulb from the earth. Cup it in your hands. What will happen now if you plant the lily bulb again? It bloomed, then died, but if you plant it in the soil once more, it will live again. This is nature's promise. The cycle of death, birth and rebirth is clearly shown to us in the world around us, but we do not always recognize it.

In winter, the earth appears dead, but does it not live again, and continue? The lily plant will die, but the life force within remains, and it will live again. The physical body is the armor our soul wears and uses in this world. Your pet's physical body may have died, but his or her soul lives, and if you cannot accept the concept that your pet will live again, you can at least know that your pet's soul, or spirit, continues.

Some depression is normal during bereavement. But deep depression can be life-threatening. Suicidal feelings are not uncommon in pet grief—the mourner may fantasize about being reunited with the deceased loved one—but such fantasies are rarely carried out. Grieving is only a trigger mechanism, not the root cause, for suicidal thoughts in individuals who have suffered previous bouts of severe depression or psychological problems. If you feel suicidal, get help. Self-destruction and repetitive mental battering are not the answer to your pain. Your pet surely would want you to be happy—to continue living and loving with his or her memory. Remember, your pet's death is not the end to your loving relationship—it is a new beginning. Reach out between this physical world and the spiritual world, and sustain your loving bond.

There is nothing wrong with seeking help from a mental health professional. There are traumatic times in life when we all need a helping hand. Getting help when you know it is needed is a sign of strength. You are giving yourself a gift of positive action, growth and resolution.

There is probably no need to seek therapy if you feel you are resolving your grief on your own. The need for professional help is usually tied to unresolved mental, physical or psychological problems that existed before your pet's death and may affect your ability to cope with grief.

Talk about your feelings with your family and friends. There is nothing to be ashamed of in admitting that you need help. Seek out a support group for pet loss (you can call the mental health hotlines in the blue pages of your telephone book). Speak with your veterinarian and ask for a referral to a support group or competent bereavement counselor. Give yourself the opportunity to benefit from the understanding and tender loving care of the people around you who want to help.

On the long, grim journey of bereavement, depression can help you move toward resolution. Quiet withdrawal can provide an opportunity to meditate on the upsetting reality suddenly confronting you. When you allow yourself time to accept your loss, you gain emotional strength and regain perspective. You will be released from sorrow and recover your ambition to go on living, recognizing that the transition of your beautiful, loving relationship with your pet is not the end. In the following chapters, you'll read about ways to memorialize your pet and take constructive action to help you resolve all of the emotions presented in this chapter.

Be strong. Have faith in yourself, as your pet always has.

3

Resolution

RESOLUTION IS UPLIFTING YOUR INNER SELF THROUGH POSITIVE action. In this final stage of grieving, you are able to release the grief and pain yet retain your pet's loving memory. You begin to heal. Your attention and emotional focus shift, allowing you to continue with your life's evolution. Your emotional suffering and pain wane, and you form an inner core of hope and self-regeneration. By preserving your beloved pet's memory, you let go of your sorrow.

You may encounter certain obstacles, however. There are physical reminders (such as your pet's toys) and other associations that cause grief to linger because they constantly remind you that your pet is no longer with you physically. Remove toys and other reminders if they upset you. (You may wish to perform the Cleansing the Gate ritual in Chapter Nine as you do this.) Once your grieving has subsided, bring the articles back out into the open.

Speak freely about your loss, and your mourning period will shorten. Releasing the pain makes room for healing, and talking about your feelings changes grief into a constructive process.

If your needs during this crucial time are not met, or if you do not complete your mourning, the suffering may continue for years, or for a lifetime. When you resist the natural process of mourning, you are hurting yourself more than the actual mourning process ever could. You need to go through the self-repair that is part of grieving. Sharing your feelings with others is kinder than shutting them out, and helps teach them how to respect and understand the grieving of pet death.

As you come to this final stage of resolution, you are letting go gradually, accepting the reality of the transition you and your pet have made, and of its altering effects on your life. You remember your loving relationship with your pet, and continue to feel intense love for him or her, understanding that although you have physically lost your pet, you remain together in memory and in spirit. You are able to go on living, and your beloved pet warms your way.

The path of grieving is one that you must walk one step at a time. Healing comes as you learn to live with the loss, the changes in your life and your loving memories. It takes time to achieve complete resolution. Don't become frustrated with yourself. This frustration can drastically slow or cripple your recovery. As you pick up the pieces, you are exercising the strength you gained from that special bond with your pet. What you make of your life now is the ultimate testimony of your shared love.

Stepping Stones toward Resolution
The following suggestions, which I call "stepping stones," may help you cope with your grief. If you feel emotionally overwhelmed, or if some suggestions do not sound right for you, pick those that are most appealing and do one step a day. Do not

force yourself to follow any of these suggestions; each should be done without resistance. Give yourself time to become ready. These are steps to ease your pain and start you on the path of resolution.

- If you must make provisions to have euthanasia administered to your pet, avoid scheduling the appointment on a holiday or a special date that could be emotionally upsetting in future years.

You should not permit yourself the stress and sadness of losing your beloved pet on a special date, such as your birthday or your pet's.

- When your pet has died, immediately make an appointment to speak with your veterinarian.

This is particularly important if you are feeling denial or guilt. You may have doubts, questions and concerns about your pet's death. Write your questions on a sheet of paper so you do not forget them during the conversation, should you become emotionally unraveled. This appointment is not to personally attack your pet's physician because you are upset or feel the veterinarian make some mistake. Ask for advice. If you pet died in veterinary care, get details about your pet's death. If there was something you did not understand earlier, bring up the issue and get answers. Your veterinarian, if a true "animal person" and a sensitive doctor, will patiently and thoroughly answer any questions and provide support.

Many people feel put off by their veterinarians. Often veterinarians and their staff will not approach a grieving individual unless sought for advice. There are good reasons for this. First, they may feel that death is a personal matter that clients will wish to resolve on their own. Second, the veterinarian and staff want to appear calm and collected when you are not. As you are falling to pieces emotionally, the veterinarian must remain capable of making arrangements for your pet's body and seeing that the proper steps are taken. In most cases, the veterinarian is not truly insensitive—he or she simply waits to be approached by a grieving client.

- Whether in the veterinary office, at the site of the death, or some days after your pet's death, it is not too late to tell your pet how much you love him or her.

Sometimes it helps to write a letter to your pet, expressing how you feel. You can include happy memories or some of the silly traits your pet displayed when alive that made you smile. Keep the letter with the other physical remembrances you have saved in tribute to your pet. Communicating with your pet during meditation sessions is also beneficial (see the Loving between the Worlds Meditation in Chapter Three).

Writing helps. Whenever you are distressed and no one is listening, you can get your point across through writing. Writing about your pet's death, or listing all the loving memories you've shared with your pet, helps to draw your feelings from within you and objectively place them before you. Recalling your memories on paper will be of great value during your mourning, and will later serve as a visible representation of your fond memories. The writing helps you cope.

Another writing exercise that can help is writing a letter to yourself from your pet. What would your pet say to you? How would your pet wish you to best cope and go on living? Some people scoff at the idea, but I assure you that this exercise can help by revealing inner truths about yourself, and will serve as a valued personal document to keep with your pet's belongings.

- Hold a service for your pet, whether it be a home burial, cemetery burial or cremation.

I have outlined rituals in Chapter Nine that can be easily conducted, and altered if necessary, to guide you in accepting the transformation for both your pet and yourself. A beautiful ritual can create positive and permanent memories to reflect upon in the future. It allows you to feel a sense of control and of providing assistance to your pet as he or she journeys into the afterlife. In some house blessings and other magical practices, we find a spirit or lost soul who needs a helping hand in reaching the other side. We take steps to help that spirit, and should show the same caring, loving gesture to our pets.

At the burial and cremation, invite only supportive, understanding and appreciative family and friends. Children should be included in the ritual planning and allowed to help carry out the ritual in some way. This stepping stone has proven to be one of the healthiest beginnings of resolution.

Although certainly a spiritual ceremony can be healing, it is not necessary. The main idea is to express your inner spiritual values in a loving manner. If family members or close friends are present and wish to be involved in the ceremony, you can speak first, then encourage them to say something they are feeling, or simply "Good-bye." If you are the only person at the ceremony, that is fine, too. In such a personal, spiritual relationship, being alone may be best.

- At home, or in private, allow yourself to cry and let your feelings come forth.

When at work, or out in public, we strive to keep calm and show no emotional strain. However, the confusion, sorrow and pain must be expressed and dealt with. Suppressing your feelings, or denying their existence, will only be harmful and slow your healing process. Also, suppressed feelings may surface in public places, where they may cause you more embarrassment and distress.

Men especially have a terrible time coping. Men are taught to be strong, not to show tears, and to control their feelings at all times. There is absolutely nothing wrong with a man who expresses his emotions. The process is normal, natural and beautiful. Remember, you need to work through your emotions or they will surface when you least expect it, and whether you want them to or not.

- Change your daily routine.

Having a pet means you have a routine. At 6:00 every morning I awaken to feed my bird and two dogs. I then take my dogs outside. I have a set schedule for my pets' walks, meals and playtime. When your pet has died, change your entire routine immediately and establish a new one. I cannot stress the importance of this enough. Three mornings in a row after my cat Louis died, I placed food in his dish. It can be very upsetting to follow the same routine, expecting to see your pet present, and then be forced to acknowledge the reality.

Get up earlier or later in the morning. Try reversing the order of some of your morning tasks. Schedule chores completely differently. Do not sit frequently on the furnishings where your pet always lay down or came to you for affection. Better yet, rearrange your furniture and decorations. There has been an enormous and emotionally stressful transformation in your life. Do not cause yourself additional or unnecessary grief by following the same routine.

- Visit with people.

I realize that you will desire privacy to mourn, but continue to visit good friends, date and see family. Talk about your grief with supportive others. If you live alone, or feel uncomfortable speaking with family or friends, attend a bereavement support group in your area. Most large towns have these. You can locate one by looking in the blue pages of your telephone book under

Mental Health Services, or by calling your veterinarian for a referral.

If you cannot leave your home due to emotional stress, invite people to visit you. If a friend or family member has a pet you especially like, or who was your pet's favorite playmate, consider having the pet to visit, too. Sometimes another pet who was friendly with your own can provide a sense of physical closeness to your pet and help you to accept the past and look forward to the future. You may even wish to visit a park with your pet's friend, or special sites you and your beloved pet enjoyed. This enables you to keep alive and relive your memories without distorting the reality you must now accept.

- Keep a journal.

Buy a notebook, or attractive stationery and a folder, and record your feelings, positive or negative. Once you've recorded them each day, never go back and change what you wrote or discard portions that don't reflect your current feelings. This journal will serve as another memorial to your pet and provide insight into your innermost feelings.

Seeking Counseling

One moment you feel in control and able to handle the psychological tension and agony of grieving. In the next moment you are unable to lift yourself from the emotional pits of mourning. When you feel no sign of improvement in your emotional state of mind, or see a loved one mired in a similar state, seek help.

In our modern society, it is difficult to become close to another human being in an unconditional, loving manner. Our pets are often closer to us than other humans. Human personalities and environmental obstacles make it hard to establish meaningful relationships with family members, friends and co-workers. It is easy to see why some people are dependent upon their animal companions.

In the increasing numbers of bereavement support groups, mental health hot lines, gay rights organizations, programs to assist the homeless and many other examples, we see that humanity is striving to help itself. It makes me smile to know that more and more people are letting go of selfishness and reaching out to help others in need. While it is clear that as a society we are experiencing many terrible difficulties, there is an evolving, positive public attitude. Individuals are changing how they look at themselves, and others, for the good.

Through this evolved sensitivity toward other people, many health care professionals and mental health practitioners now realize that grieving for one's pet, as well as for a beloved human, is valid.

When you cannot cope, you need to share your grief and find positive counsel. Seeking trained help indicates that you are a strong, mentally healthy individual who recognizes when help is needed. It is possible that as you grieve for your pet, you could subconsciously be suffering from a personal problem or an unresolved, previous death, whether of a person or another pet. If you are unable to overcome depression or resolve your emotions, there may be cause for concern. If you feel that this description fits your situation, or a family member or close friend makes a similar judgment, then you may choose to seek professional therapy to help you cope.

The acceptance and availability of pet grief counseling have spread in recent years. Most American households have pets, so the death of a beloved pet is a common experience for many of us. However, there may be limited resources of pet bereavement counseling in your area. Ask your veterinarian for a referral to a counselor or support group.

When searching on your own for a bereavement counselor, do so carefully. There exist unscrupulous individuals who enter this industry for financial gain, and some have little interest in offering true help. Ask for references. Speak to the counselor's past clientele—call the references on the list and ask if they felt helped. This action in itself will provide you with sensitive, sympathetic contacts who can help you at this critical time. You may make new friends in the process. Ask a counselor or therapist for proof of credentials, especially if the practitioner requires a fee for service.

At the end of this book, you'll find a list of centers that provide pet bereavement counseling. If the listed contacts are not convenient, write or call them to ask if they can direct you to a resource in your area.

Spiritual Communication toward Resolution

Resolution is a beautiful stage. You retain the memories of your blessed time with your pet, yet the suffering has disappeared. The beauty of your unique bond with your pet is that the loving relationship does not end at death, but changes to a spiritual one. You have your pet with you here in the physical world always, until the glorious reunion you will have in spirit. Your pet's memory and love will bring you happiness for the rest of your life—then beyond. This is true love.

When I speak to you of the new, spiritual relationship you have with your pet, I refer to the love and communication that are possible between you, here in the physical world, and your pet, or any deceased loved one, in the spirit world. In our culture, we feel we have to "see it to believe it," and this is very sad because the hidden realities are so important to our happiness. The fact that your pet has physically died does not mean that his or her soul, or spirit, does not exist. All living creatures have a soul, or spirit, which continues after death and eventually is reborn. Your pet exists in spirit, and the love between you has not changed. Enjoy the love that lives on in your transformed relationship.

It is through ritual work that communication with the deceased is possible. There are various ways to interact with your loved ones, including your pet. Meditation leading to trance, the talking board, the pendulum board, crystal ball gazing and many acts of channeling can prompt this communication. All of these techniques can be effective for communication with your pet now in the spirit world.

Depending upon your personal spiritual beliefs, it is often thought that deceased pets are spiritual ties to the other world. It is common for the deceased pet to remain closely in contact with the human loved one, even taking on the role of spirit guide, helping both of you toward further spiritual growth. A simple meditation ritual can bridge our physical world and the spiritual world. Experiencing the bridge and meeting your pet on the other side can deepen your already-existing bond. The loving connection through the bridge of communication is beautiful and empowering as you reach resolution.

Loving between the Worlds Meditation
Sessions of communication with your pet can be as frequent as you desire and are beautiful exercises of love for both of you. Though the energy-based interaction will be different from the physical relationship you experienced before, it has its own beauty, sensations and ways to exchange love.

Through this spiritual dedication to your pet, you may feel a redirection of your life. The joy, learning and exchange of love you experienced in living with your pet have enriched your life and will benefit you forever.

What You'll Need
- White flowers, candles and crystals to decorate your sacred space (these articles are optional; choose decorations you are comfortable with, including your pet's belongings)
- Matches
- Incense to help obtain a meditative state (sweetgrass is ideal, as it is often used to draw spirits)
- Quiet music, if desired

Preparations

For this and the other meditations described in this book, you may wish to read the instructions into a tape recorder, with pauses where you will need time to carry them out. Rather than stopping your meditation to consult this text, you may prefer to play the recording.

Decorate a table to use as an altar, or create a sanctuary for your pet, using the flowers, candles, crystals and other personal objects.

Dress in a ritual robe or comfortable clothing.

Darken your private sacred space, using the candles for illumination.

Use the procedures of your religious practice to open. This may mean reciting the Lord's Prayer, summoning the four elements or other rituals, depending on your spiritual path.

Lie flat on your back with your legs bent and your feet on the floor. Relax every part of your body, starting with your feet and ending with your head. Tense and relax each muscle group to ensure total body relaxation. Repeat if necessary. Feel grounded through the pressure of your feet against the earth. Feel the energy moving upward from your feet, through your entire being, and exiting at the top of your head. You are centered and deeply relaxed.

Meditate, allowing your conscious mind to rest as deeper levels of your unconscious mind unfold. Focus your will on communicating with your beloved pet. When you feel ready, ask your pet to appear to you.

If you experience a block when attempting to communicate with your pet, ask for his or her help. Draw energy up from the earth, through your feet, and release it through the top of your head, to prompt clarity within your aura.

When your pet appears, look at him or her. What does your pet look like? Is he or she in bodily form or in an energy form? Ask what he or she needs from you. Ask how it is easiest for you to contact him or her. Are there other beings present with your pet—other animals, spirit guides or angels? Is there someone else who wishes to come forward to communicate with you? Ask whatever questions you wish to have answered at this initial communication. Provide time between each question for your pet to send you messages in answer. The communication process should be slow paced.

Once you've asked your initial questions and communicated with your pet long enough, send love through your aura and say a temporary farewell. Come out of the meditation slowly. Return gently, allowing your conscious mind to awaken.

Offer thanks to your deity for making the communication with your beloved pet possible. You may wish to ground yourself by eating food. You may even decide to have a snack within your sacred space and reflect on your wonderful interaction with your pet.

Creating a Memorial
Planning your pet's funeral proceedings and meditating to cope with your grief are steps on the path to emotional balance. Your

tears of sorrow are replaced by peaceful acceptance, understanding and an eternal love for your pet that becomes a tool in achieving resolution of your grief.

You regain stamina and begin to feel strong again. You are reminded of your pet's belongings temporarily stored away, and feel the desire to bring them out of storage to memorialize him or her.

Following are some ideas for making a memorial shelf or other memorial space within your home. In crafting a shelf, or planning a memorial section within a bookcase or on a table top, you are expressing your undying love and acknowledging that you must continue with your life, enjoying the memory of your pet and honoring your spiritual relationship with him or her.

Look for spaces within your home to display your pet's belongings. Clear a shelf in a glass-encased china cabinet and place your pet's belongings there, with photos and memorabilia. Clear off and dust a decorative shelf in your living room or dining room and display your pet's photo, favorite toys, or his or her cremation urn, should you choose that final arrangement. In my living room, I have a small wooden shelf that holds photos of my two beloved cats, who were buried. When my Miniature Spitz, Sasha, died of cancer, I had her cremated and placed her ashes on the shelf, too, with a photo.

Many people prefer their pet's memorial shelf or space to be in the bedroom, so that they can speak to their beloved pet at night or have privacy with his or her spirit whenever desired. Other people choose a room in the home where their pet enjoyed sitting in the sun, or played with the children. If you have children, it is considerate to discuss the memorial with them and allow them to choose the location. Frequently, the spot chosen will be in the living room, where the entire family can remember the beloved pet together.

Memorializing your pet is not silly, though some insensitive people might think so. A woman I met once told me she had made a memorial under her bed for her poodle who had died of cancer. She said her husband scoffed at her grief and joked about her keeping her poodle's biker jacket and other belongings. Secretly, she placed all her pet's belongings, and many letters of love, into a decorative, zippered pillow she had made herself. For years the memorial pillow has been under her side of the bed, and she opens it on occasion to this day to enjoy the sweet memories it holds.

There are several other ideas—like making a scrapbook for your pet. You can include photos, your journal, and your pet's collars, leash, and tags. My neighbor, a teenage girl, wears her dog's tag on a necklace around her neck. She says one day she will place it in her jewelry box, but not until she is ready.

Deciding what favorite toys, photos and other items will be included is healthy for children as well as adults. The process reminds you that your pet is with you in spirit and always accessible to you through memory. You can paint or decorate your shelf as you feel is appropriate. I saw an attractive shelf in a client's home that had each family member's name painted around the pet's name in different colors—it looked very charming and the children loved the idea. Whether you choose to purchase a furnishing for your pet's memorabilia or to construct one, you will find that the gesture makes you feel much better emotionally and preserves the physical love you shared with your pet.

At a cemetery or home burial, you can have a grave marker or dedication plaque made in memory of your pet. You can have a portrait of your pet painted by an artist to hang in your home in remembrance. If your pet is cremated, you can purchase an urn with a plaque, or make a decorative holder for your pet's ashes. Many animal rescue and human organizations accept donations in your pet's name, and may even place your name and your pet's name on a large appreciation plaque. In donating, you know your love for your pet is being extended toward the well-being and rescue of other animals—future pets that may touch someone's heart as much as your pet touches yours.

Each of us has a unique, loving bond with our pet. It is a beautiful act of love to memorialize your pet, no matter what means you choose. You will also feel stronger and happier, and start healing.

4

Bereavement and Children

CHILDREN AND PETS SHARE A SIBLING-LIKE BOND. IN MANY households, the family considers their pet a family member. There is nothing unusual about this. When your child is sad, a pet can provide comfort as a best friend and closest companion. If your child misbehaves and you scold, the family pet is a friend who will listen to the child's side of the story. When you are busy or unable to spend time with your child, a pet can give your child a sense of security and continuity. When your child is teased or tormented by bullies at school, or feels unable to fit in with peers, a pet provides a friendship of pure acceptance and love, without judgment or criticism. And at night, if your child becomes frightened by shadows or by monsters in the closet, the family pet can cuddle and comfort the child to sleep.

Through the growing relationship with his or her pet, your child learns love and trust, develops responsibility and gains self-esteem. These experiences influence your child's growing personality and attitude in life. In an overwhelming or confusing world, your child's pet is a living symbol of his or her emotional security.

It is a shame that a child's sadness at the death of a pet is not taken as seriously as it should be by our society. The emotional turmoil a child feels at a pet's death can be overwhelming. As adults, we attempt to protect children from grief, because we consider it an adult problem that they should not have to deal with. But as we attempt to deal with the busyness of our own lives, we can easily trivialize a child's loss and fail to give the respect, understanding and loving attention that he or she desperately needs.

For parents, the topic of death is as uncomfortable to explain as the "birds and the bees" lecture is to deliver. We dread facing our children's pain and their difficult questions about death. Meanwhile, we are struggling to deal with our own grief. Thinking that children are too immature intellectually to perceive what is really happening, we may decide not to share our feelings of sorrow with our children. But children are very intuitive. When adults mourn a death and exclude their children, the children may wonder, "Why won't Mom and Dad tell me what is wrong?" Your child knows when you are upset and when he or she is excluded from important family matters. When they believe you don't trust them enough to tell them why you are upset, children can feel ashamed and guilty, and may wonder what they did to cause you to exclude them.

When a human loved one dies, younger children are often not allowed to attend funerals, wakes and burials. Parents sometimes keep their children from visiting an individual who is dying. But death is a part of life. There are many situations in life that are uncomfortable and frightening, but education makes the difference. It is my opinion that the natural act of mourning needs to be allowed for children.

The bereavement of pet loss will help your child learn healthy ways of resolution that will be of benefit later in adult life. He or she will be better prepared to cope with death in the future when early experiences provide a healthy, realistic understanding. You are your child's guide, and you need to share in the learning and healing process. Once your child has realized the feeling of loss and grief, you need to be supportive and available to answer your child's curious and heartfelt questions.

Talking about Death

Regardless of your child's age, sooner or later the experience of death will be felt. Your child will hear about death on television, in movies, at school, from friends and during your conversations when you think he or she is not paying attention. Despite this, he or she may recognize that death is not a subject openly talked about. When your child first experiences a personal loss, how do you begin to explain? What should your child know or not know? How can you best explain without upsetting your child further?

As parents and adults, we have an obligation to begin a child's education about death in a constructive manner. A child's response to death is more unconditioned and curious than an adult's. Education about death as an inevitable part of life can be a growth experience and an occasion for positive enlightenment.

If your child's pet is diagnosed with sickness or injury that will result in death, you need to attempt to discuss pet death and grief with your child right away, before the pet dies. You may be surprised at your child's willingness and awareness in discussing terminal illness or injury and death. When your family pet is ill or

injured and a decision must be made to apply euthanasia, you
need to include children in the decision-making process. This can
be painful and upsetting, but it helps to bring forth emotions that
may otherwise be suppressed or not understood. Explain why you
feel you have made the right decision, and share your feelings.
Young children who can't articulate do not necessarily have to sit
in on the decision making, but you do need to inform them of
where their pet is going, and why.

Many adults talk with their children about death to reassure
them that their pet will experience rebirth, or at least that the
pet's spirit continues. If your child is of an age to understand, you
may wish to share and discuss in an elementary way theories
concerning the afterlife and what happens at physical death. One
idea is to use a "fairy tale format" for younger children. Telling a
story addressing death that involves your spiritual beliefs can help
your child best understand that death is a part of life, and that a
Divine Source—a god, goddess, angel, creator—is watching over
his or her pet in the afterlife. This is a suitable introduction to
death, and provides a sense of security that the pet is safe in the
afterlife, yet remains with your child in spirit and memory.

It is often better to avoid any morbid details about the pet's
death, autopsy and other physical matters. These facts may
frighten your child. Keeping the physical details to a minimum
will help your child understand death in a more positive way.

Try to answer your child's questions in a simple way, but do
not oversimplify. "FiFi went on a long trip" or "Jake was sick and
had to go away" is not a positive, constructive explanation. Your
intention may be to protect your child, but when the child grows

to realize the truth, such vague euphemisms will seem a betrayal and a lie. The incident could create feelings of anger, mistrust, resentment and worry. It is not uncommon for negative childhood experiences, particularly when a child feels greatly wronged, to resurface emotionally later in life.

Proceed carefully. Hoping your child will forget about a pet's death is unreasonable. Do we ever truly forget? If you avoid discussing the issue, your child's stress may be expressed through problems in daily activities, or physical and emotional symptoms, such as depression, poor performance in school, misconduct and nightmares.

If you have a problem coping with death, you will have trouble explaining death to your child in a comfortable and reassuring way. Remember that children are accepting and resilient, and that what we as adults perceive as unthinkable or horrible may go unconsidered by a child, who may not fully understand all the components of the situation. Of utmost importance is that you do not lie or ignore your child's questions or concerns. If you become upset yourself, explain your feelings to your child. If you do not, your child may feel he or she has done something to upset you.

Suggestions

The best way to begin the discussion is to ask your child what he or she thinks death is. Your child may have a confused idea of death, based on cartoon shows or other influences. Or he or she may surprise you with a very perceptive answer. From your child's answer you can determine how much to explain, and how to do it. Use a simple and straightforward explanation, and your child will more fully understand what has happened and that the feelings of grief are normal and natural.

Ask questions to get feedback from your child. "Max was sick, and he died. Do you know what death is?" You can also use a statement like the following to reassure your child that his or her feelings are natural and you are there to help: "I know you hurt and miss Max, but I want you to know that I understand your feelings and will help you if you have questions." Work on your child's level by gauging what upsets or confuses him or her regarding the pet's death.

The response to pet loss differs from child to child, depending upon age and intellectual development. Your child's grief may range from seemingly nonexistent to severe, and parents can be shocked by an unexpected response. In all cases, death needs to be explained with reassurance—not as something bad or to be feared. Acknowledge to your child that death can be extremely upsetting, and that his or her response is natural.

It is easy for adults to become impatient with a small child's repetitive statements of "But I want him back," or "Why can't I see him?" Younger children may not be able to intellectually accept or understand death. Your patience and gentle explaining is needed as they struggle to comprehend what has happened.

Jokes, humor and belittling a child's very real emotional upset will only cause the child more suffering, shame, guilt and pain. It is possible that adults who scoff at mourning the loss of a pet may do so because as children they never received compassionate understanding of bereavement. Their parents may have ignored their questions, refused to discuss the subject or otherwise made death seem either trivial or unspeakable. These children may have grown into insensitive adults who do not know how to be compassionate toward pet bereavement. If you trivialize your child's grief, you risk sending a powerful message: "This is how I would act if you died." Allow your child to sense how you respond and truly feel regarding the pet's death. Your example will provide answers, and your child will feel secure and positive. This is the ultimate goal.

It is helpful to share your positive religious views and spirituality with your child. It is a topic that can make the discussion easier and give your child a feeling of further support. It helps to talk about nature's changing seasons, how the earth is reborn in the spring, thrives in summer and fall and "dies" in winter. It can be a great example of how birth, death and rebirth are part of the cycle of life. Use ideology your child is capable of understanding and will find comforting.

With children who have been religiously taught, there is always the chance that they might think that the gods are punishing them for some offense by taking their beloved pet. Spiritual guidance coupled with death education will help your child overcome this misconception.

I see nothing wrong with telling children that their pet is "with God/Goddess," or "living with angels." Once you have explained death and afterlife, it is common for children to wonder precisely where their pet is, and with whom.

Your child must benefit from your example. You are the primary role model. Treat his or her grief seriously and share your feelings. Take care, proceed gently, and answer your child's questions as best you can. Your discussions of pet loss and death with your child may help him or her cope better with a human loved one's death in the future.

Where Is My Pet Now?

How can we answer such questions when we don't have precise answers, and we know the answers we do have may hurt? Our hearts ache when we are asked, because we feel our child's uncertainty and pain.

Children ask many questions about where their pet has gone, whether the pet is happy being dead, whether God or Goddess takes care of the pet now and—for me, the most difficult question—"Will I ever see my pet again?" You must assess exactly what your child means by a question to provide proper guidance. When a young child asks this last question, he or she is usually referring to this life. Answering "I don't know" leaves your child feeling lost and confused. While you honestly may not know, you need to try to provide answers that will satisfy the origin of the question and ease your child's mind.

There are times when your child may ask another adult the same questions and acquire different answers. If this should happen, you can explain that many people have different beliefs about death and the afterlife, and that you have told your child what you believe to be correct. We all may have different beliefs, but we can agree that death is not an end, but a transition.

It is best to inform other family members and friends of what you have told your child regarding death and grief. Other adults mean no harm but may provide unsuitable answers, not knowing how best to respond.

Your child may be unable to understand the concept of rebirth or heaven. He or she may disagree with your explanation and adopt another. What's important is that your child have a comforting answer. Accept your child's beliefs, and adjust your discussion to include them.

Certain explanations are commonly misinterpreted by children and should be avoided. Some of these are: your pet got sick and died (without further explanation, or if untrue), your pet went to sleep forever, your pet ran away from home (if untrue), the gods loved your pet so much that they wanted him or her back, your pet wanted to be free and wild, and many more. I am sure you can understand the negative results of these answers and why they should not be used.

The child whose pet simply "got sick and died" may worry that everyone close to him or her who falls ill is likely to die. This can create a phobia. You need to explain further.

Being told, "Your pet went to sleep" means to your child that sleeping can result in death. A phobia can result.

Children can become suspicious if you tell them untruthfully that their pet ran away. Your child will either realize you are being dishonest, or wait in agony for the pet to return. This creates feelings of exclusion, betrayal and worry.

Telling your child that the gods wanted the pet back causes the child to wonder why he or she has not been taken back as well, or to worry that he or she, or loved ones, will be suddenly snatched away.

Another common answer is that your child's pet had to be put to sleep because of illness or injury. This prompts questions of how, when and why. Your child may begin to fear doctors and medical procedures. Imagine an anesthesiologist lifting a gas mask to your child's face and saying, "Now you'll sleep for a time." Children understand things literally. They generally cannot fully understand the use of metaphors.

Don't shy away from crying and grieving if you suddenly feel tears coming on. Children need to be sensitized to other people's emotions.

Your child will trust you even more when you confirm that what they feel is real, and pay attention to their confusion and pain. For the rest of your child's life, your relationship will benefit from your gentle guidance at this sensitive time.

Constructive Coping for Your Child

There are actions you can take to help ease your child through the painful ordeal of grief. In Chapter Nine I offer the "Crossing The Bridge" funeral ritual to help soothe your own grief and your child's, along with healthy meditation techniques and other exercises to help you and your child cope.

To help your child adjust to the death of a beloved pet, you might try stimulating joyful reminiscing. Using photographs can help. Make a point to tell your child that through remembering the pet and cherishing the special love they shared, the pet will continue to be a part of his or her life.

Encourage your child to write a letter to the pet. This allows your child to express his or her grief and longing for the pet. If you choose to make a scrapbook or photo album with your child, the letters your child may write can be placed inside as well.

Making a memorial shelf or sanctuary to your pet in your home can help your child maintain a physical attachment. Your child may visit the memorial and talk openly to the pet. This is healthy and positive.

Children sometimes pretend that their pet is with them, and who is to say that in spirit the pet is not? This action is healthy and beneficial, and helps your child cope.

A trip to the library might be in order to assist you in explaining the subject of death. There are wonderful children's books available on the subject. Whether it comes from you or not, it is important your child receive some form of education and answers to his or her questions.

You can telephone your veterinarian and ask if he or she can take a few minutes to talk with your child about the pet's death. This is an especially good idea if your child knows the pet died while at the veterinary clinic. The veterinarian can sometimes handle the hard-to-answer questions in an informed and gentle manner.

One of the most positive and helpful actions you can take is to have a funeral or burial ceremony for your child's pet. You can help your child understand the transition he or she is experiencing in the physical loss of the pet, a process that can bring you closer together. Your child will be strengthened by the family's shared rites that acknowledge death as a part of life.

A pet's death can cause emotional problems in even the most well-adjusted child. Your child will look to people of authority, particularly you, for words of wisdom and guidance. You might inform your child's teacher about the death and ask for advice on guiding your child. At the least, your child's teacher should be notified in case your child should suffer some hardships participating in classroom activities, or seem troubled. The teacher may even take the opportunity to discuss pets and pet loss during class, not only to help other children become aware of what your child is going through, but also to further much-needed positive attention to the subject. Only goodness can evolve from such discussion.

Any constructive discussion and action you can provide for your child will increase his or her trust and bond with you. Taking steps to help your child cope, and working together on fun pet memorializing projects, reinforces your role as your child's loving guide through all the emotional trials and triumphs in his or her young life.

5

Pet Loss through Terminal Illness

EVERY LIVING CREATURE IS SUSCEPTIBLE TO TERMINAL ILLNESS; IN our lives we will know and love many people and animals who will experience it. The relentless advance of disease challenges your loving relationship with your pet, and the battle to preserve your pet's life creates emotional and physical demands that are born of love and hope.

Universal in pet bereavement is the feeling that you have lost control. You feel you have failed in your responsibility in caring for your pet. You may feel guilt or blame for your pet's disease, but in your heart you know that neither is just—you have done your best with the medical and scientific knowledge available to you to nurture and protect your pet.

Through visits to your veterinarian, you provide health screening and medical care for your pet, assuming that these will defeat disease. When a pet is found to have a terminal illness, you may blame the veterinarian for not discovering the disease earlier. You logically know that cancer and other terminal illnesses are silent killers that in many cases show no early symptoms. In your desperation to hold onto your beloved pet, however, your sensitive emotions may overcome your logical understanding.

The onset of terminal illness often goes unnoticed until the disease has progressed and cannot be controlled. Your initial shock may be followed by feelings of excessive guilt that cause you to blame yourself or others. You must consider that the progression of terminal illness in pets is similar to disease in our own species. Medical research, vaccines, tests and treatments may prolong the quality of life, but they cannot conquer disease. Preventive medicine is the best measure we can take to prolong health, vitality and life for ourselves and loved ones.

If your veterinarian informs you of your pet's terminal illness, remember that it is a moment of distress for the medical care provider as well. Devoted veterinarians are animal lovers themselves, and having to be a messenger of death is agonizing for them. Your veterinarian may feel a sense of failure, guilt and sorrow. We often have preconceived notions that our health professionals are emotionally callused and can no longer feel such distress. We may also wrongfully think of our physicians as godlike—holding the fate of our pet in their hands—and expect more of them than realistically can be given.

Your love for your pet, and your willingness to suffer emotional, psychological, physical and financial hardship for his or her benefit, is no competition against an invisible killer. The harsh reality is that blood transfusions, radiation and other medical action to fight terminal illness does not often result in a cure. Your pet's life may be prolonged, but you will need to accept that no cure exists. It is important at this time to consider the quality of life of both you and your pet. It is common in cases of terminal illness for pet lovers to suffer loss of quality of life through emotional breakdown and financial poverty. You cannot benefit your pet by sustaining his or her life when his or her quality of life, or yours, has dissolved to the point of no recovery.

Your veterinarian may recommend options that can prolong your pet's life, with a good chance of a cure or at least a comfortable existence. If your veterinarian cannot offer any such hope, seek a second opinion, but be prepared for the possibility that there may be no cure.

The most difficult moments in our lives occur when we have the responsibility of deciding whether another creature lives or dies. Loved ones, human and animal, depend upon us to make the right decision without hesitation. It is common for an adult to write a living will or specify whether or not life support should be used in case of terminal illness or injury. Our pets are unable to specify their desires, so we can only judge what is best by their behavior, physical condition and apparent quality of life. Our selfish tendencies in not wanting to be without the love and life of a pet can cause our pets to suffer unnecessarily; we must ensure that our intentions are to benefit our pets and not ourselves. We can agree that no living creature should be forced to live in pain and suffering. Perhaps the easiest way to determine the best decision is to reverse roles with your pet. If you were suffering the diagnosed terminal illness, what would you prefer family members, including your pet, to decide? (See Chapter Six for further information and advice.)

Family Discussion

The day your veterinarian tells you of your pet's terminal illness, inform other family members, especially children. Explain the terminal illness and possible consequences to your children in terms they can understand. It may help if children are encouraged to speak directly to the veterinarian providing your pet's treatment. Children must be allowed to ask questions, and receive sensible answers. Often, their fantasies about what is happening are worse than the reality. Inform children about the illness, not only to prepare them for the coming death, but also to warn them that the pet may no longer be able to play. Suddenly grabbing or playing too rough with a sick pet can result in injury to both pet and child. Of course, it is not fair to scold your child for playing with the family pet without explaining why. Children need to understand that their pet is very ill, and that provisions must be made to make the pet comfortable. Children can be wonderful care providers when notified of another living creature's plight. Informing them promptly will give them a head start on coping with the grieving process.

In family discussion of a pet's terminal illness, it is common for disputes to arise. When medical options are available, the family unit may split. Children and other family members may prefer the pet to remain in the home and receive treatment, even if there is no medical hope. Parents may disagree on the proper action. Financial and emotional factors, coupled with disagreements regarding the pet's quality of life, are usually the cause for disputes.

In talking with your family, let children share their preferences, and answer their questions as best you can. If you know that there is no medical hope and that the suggested treatments cannot be undertaken for financial or other reasons, explain this to your child. End the discussion on a positive note— reminding your child to cherish and enjoy these moments with the family pet. (See Chapter Four for more suggestions on talking to children about death and pet loss, and introducing constructive ways of coping for the family as a whole.)

If you seek the advice of others, be prepared for differences of opinion. Some pet lovers believe that once a pet is diagnosed with terminal illness, he or she should be relieved of the possibility of suffering. Other pet lovers believe that you should do everything in your power to keep your pet alive, even if it means taking a second mortgage on your home or traveling to an animal medical center thousands of miles away. Remember that each individual has an internal sense of what limits and degrees of action are appropriate. Never take the advice of another person simply because you fear judgment or condemnation of your own preference, or if your instincts tell you that the advice is incorrect. Seeking advice of several individuals, however, does have the benefit of providing different viewpoints and highlighting various concerns, especially if you are so emotionally distraught that you are unable to think clearly.

Make a decision you will agree with in the future. The moments you spend with your sick pet are filled with sorrow. You look into the twinkling eyes of your precious companion, feeling unable to determine the best decision. Any final choice is correct when based upon the essence of love. Through the essence of love, we as humans have the ability to release loved ones from the anguish of pain and suffering. Our ability to make such a decision should be considered a divine gift, not a curse. Nearly every religion on earth is based upon love, faith and charity to our fellow creatures. You can prepare yourself for the decision making through spirituality and faith, and the charity you provide through love for your pet.

Obsessing

Aside from the hardship of decision making, obsessing can be the worst torment you endure. The mental monster of obsessing is a self-inflicted preoccupation with your pet's well-being, caused by your fear of losing your pet, in combination with your heightened emotional state.

When a guarantee of death presents itself to us in the form of a terminal disease or other life-threatening source, we cannot help but focus upon the irreversible consequence. With each passing minute of the day we are continuously reminded that our pet's limited time is slipping away. Every moment with our beloved pet is shadowed by the coming loss of life, and by the time when we will no longer be able to physically express our loving bond.

Obsession creates a very dismal environment for you and your pet, and makes it nearly impossible to function in daily activities and responsibilities. You need to overcome your constant focus upon the undesirable aspects of the situation to enjoy these last moments with your beloved pet and celebrate the physical love between you. Since time can never be recaptured, you need to convince yourself to stop obsessing and celebrate your loving relationship with your pet while there is still time. Let go of the thought of death, and spend free moments exchanging expressions of love with your pet. Begin a healthy transition for your pet into the afterlife and start yourself upon the difficult pathway of acceptance and grief.

If you do not let go of obsessive thoughts, you may regret not having focused your thoughts and attention on your pet while he or she was still living. Your intention is better focused upon your shared love and enjoyment of the time you still have together. Spend as much time with your pet as possible, to make his or her transition comfortable and full of love. Release your mind from what will be. Your pet is with you now—make this time count.

Preparation through Ritual

Celebrating the bounty of love between you and your pet during the time that remains can be enhanced for you both through ritual. Unlike the rituals and meditations described later in this book, you conduct this ceremony while your pet is still living. The ritual can best be described as an initiation rite and a preparation for the transformation of your pet's spirit for its future ascendance to divinity. It celebrates the time when your pet will be free of the pain, suffering and challenges of physical existence. Blessing your pet through the power and divine love of your deity helps to prepare you both for the transition to come.

If you have not experienced the intimate interaction with your pet in the sacred space of your spiritual practices, you are missing a truly special occasion. The Spiritual Transformation Ritual described below allows you to rejoice in this experience.

Spiritual Transformation Ritual for You and Your Pet
The purpose of this ritual is to gently assist you in enjoying the remaining moments with your pet. In order to ready yourself for the ritual, you need to forget, for a time, the physical preparation for your pet's death and the decision making that will surround it—the possibility of euthanasia, the final arrangements and future action. Now is the time for acceptance, love and nurturing, for preparing within the higher self to start walking with your pet the pathway that crosses the threshold into death. You begin the transition through balance of emotion, spirit, body and mind. You and your pet face this divine transition as one in your loving bond.

This ritual may be performed alone or with other family members or friends. If you include friends or family, plan the ritual with them. Give participants an opportunity to speak, light the incense, purify the sacred space, and anoint your pet. Participants should dress comfortably and be allowed time for self-preparation.

Ideally, this ritual should be conducted outdoors, surrounded by the bounty of nature, upon the soil of our Mother Earth and beneath the heavens. Realistically, this is not always possible—especially if your pet is very ill.

What You'll Need
- An altar
- Colored cloth (see the color and attribute chart for suggestions)

- A bowl
- Candles
- Incense (frankincense and myrrh are ideal) and a censer
- A cup of water
- A cup of soil
- A spoonful of salt (the salt and water will be mixed together, or you may use holy water)
- Wine, juice, water or other natural drink of your choice, and drinking vessels, one for each participant
- A large or small cauldron or cup
- Anointing oil (I recommend cypress, because it is an oil specifically used for healing, easing losses and smoothing transitions, as well as administering protection to pets.[1] Inhalation of this oil provides an astringent scent of solace, comfort, and strength. You can find this oil at your local health food or New Age store.)
- A scarf or light cloth (lightweight or sheer and not too large—refer to the color and attribute chart below for color suggestions)
- Soft music, if desired, to accompany the ritual

General Preparations

Begin to prepare yourself early on the scheduled day. Pamper yourself with a long, relaxing bath to balance your mind and body. Through this trying time you deserve relaxing moments to tend to your own fragile state of being.

You can dress in a ritual robe or casual, comfortable clothing, as you feel is appropriate.

No special preparation for your pet is necessary. There is no reason to put your pet through a ritual bathing or grooming. If your pet is too weak to be included in the ritual activity, let him or her stay in a room nearby. Your pet should not be stressed by the ritual activity if he or she is unable to endure it. Sometimes a pet is spooked by the strange scents, the change in your voice and gestures and the unusual ritual furnishings.

Place an altar in the center of your sacred space. The altar represents the cosmos, universal energies, the earth, yourself and your spiritual beliefs. Decorate your altar with candles and a colored cloth of your choice. You can mix colors to symbolize many attributes of the ritual and the bond between you and your pet, or your altar cloth, candles and assorted decorations can be one color that intimately symbolizes the aim of your ritual. The chart below outlines some examples.

Color	Attributes
Rose or red	Love, strength, vitality
White or crystal	Peace, purification, the higher self
Gold or yellow	Divinity; energizes transformation and protects
Silver or gray	Allows receptivity to transformation
Black	Supports transformation and absorbs fears
Brown	Allows connection to nature's energies
Green	Intuition, healing, abundance

Blue   Oneness, calm, perception, wisdom
Purple   Guidance and spiritual
                             transformation

Place the cup or small cauldron on the altar. Fill it with water. The scarf or light cloth is a symbol of your pet's gradual ascent through the veil between the physical and spiritual worlds. It is a symbol of the universe or cosmic law. Place it at the front and center of your altar.

Use the procedures of your religious practice to open.

The ritual script of sacred words is divided between two participants. Formulate the wording to accommodate other participants, or, if you are alone, speak all the words yourself. The outline is a guide; change it to meet your customs or religious practices.

Gather the participants and your pet in the designated sacred space. If indoors, shut off telephones and other appliances to avoid interruption.

If your pet is present, allow him or her to lie where he or she chooses. If your pet wanders the area during the ritual, do not scold. Allow your pet to act naturally. Be careful, however, that your pet does not injure himself or herself during the ritual.

Conduct the opening ceremony, such as a prayer, of your religious practice.

Participant 1 steps before the altar and announces:

"We are gathered on this day to celebrate our loving bond with (pet's name), as he/she embarks upon the path ever nearing the threshold into death. He/she walks this path not alone, but accompanied by an abundance of love and strength, and the eternal presence of us all who cherish him/her."

Participant 2 approaches the altar and takes the cup of soil into his or her hand, pointing it upward to the sky while speaking these words:

"I invoke the presence of our Lord, that He may descend into this sacred space to both witness and bless this rite held in (pet's name)'s honor. May our Lord open the celestial gates into divinity and prepare for the coming of our beloved. Hail, O Father of all creatures great and small!"

Participant 1 takes the cup or cauldron of water into both hands, (or, if using a large cauldron, stands over it with arms raised to the sky, or to the open window). Gazing lovingly into the rippling water, he or she proclaims:

"I invoke the presence of our Lady, that She descend into this sacred space to both witness and bless this rite held in (pet's name)'s honor. May She eagerly await the coming of our beloved at the threshold between the physical and spiritual worlds as he/she gradually ascends the pathway into the afterlife. Hail, O Mother of all creatures great and small!"

Participant 2 places the cup of soil back on the altar. Participant 1 places the vessel of water back on the altar (if a large cauldron, he or she bows to it).

The salt and water are mixed together by both participants, or holy water is used. The mixture should be contained in one bowl or the cup. One of the participants sprinkles the purifying mixture around the sacred space, ending with a very light, careful sprinkle onto the pet. As this is done, sacred words are spoken:

"Our beloved (pet name) balances upon the thread between our world and that of the divine spirits. Sorrow fills our hearts, but in sorrow there is great joy in knowing our beloved will soon be free of pain and suffering. In our celebration of the union to come, of our beloved with the Lord, there is the ever-present grief for our loss.

"With the salt and water, I purify our sacred space and (pet name), in the name of (your deity), in preparation and blessing for his/her transition to come."

The salt and water container is returned to the altar once the purification is done.

The participants take the censer, circle the sacred space slowly and wave the flowing incense smoke to purify, while speaking these words:

> "We embrace the time remaining with our beloved pet in both celebration and grief: celebration of our beloved's freedom from the plights of physical existence, and grief for the loss of a cherished companion and life partner. With this holy incense, I purify the sacred space in which we have gathered to commence the inevitable journey of our beloved."

Once the incense has been circled around the sacred space, it is placed upon the altar. Incense smoke may be waved over your pet's body, but take care to avoid inhalation; do not wave it into your pet's face, or near his or her head.

Participant 1 takes the anointing oil, and, if the pet is present, he or she kneels at the pet's side. If the pet is in another area, the participant should go to the pet and anoint one, light drop on the top of the pet's head, between the ears, stating:

> "Our beloved travels upon the star-glittered heavens. Destined is our beloved for the divinity of heaven, where his/her pleasures and wants are eternally granted. Let us not shed tears of sorrow and heartache; let us shed tears of happiness and comfort in knowing that our beloved will soon be free from illness and pain. Let us not dwell on the

loss of life and physical presence, but rejoice now, through affection, in the loving bond we eternally share.

"With this anointing oil, I bless (pet name) in the name of (your deity). You shall enter the realm of death gently, shedding the physical shell that now ails you. You shall journey with strength and comfort. You are cherished now in your physical presence, and forever shall be when transformed into spirit."

Your pet is anointed carefully. The oil vessel is returned to the altar. Participant 2 takes the sheer cloth or light fabric from the altar. If two participants are present, each should grab two corners of the cloth, allowing the cloth to sag so that it almost flows. Walking slowly, so as not to frighten your pet, approach him or her and stand with the fabric held above your pet, stating:

"This cloth is symbolic of the veil between the physical and spiritual worlds. Take note of those who cherish you and embrace you in unconditional love, as we walk to the threshold of the worlds at your side. Fear not, our beloved, for we will forever be with you in spirit."

The veil is lowered and softly swept over your pet's body. Do not cover your pet entirely with the cloth, as it might frighten him or her. The "sweep" is symbolic of your pet's spirit crossing the threshold from physical existence into the afterlife of the spirit world. As the sweep is made, the following words may be spoken:

"Bound by love, trust and devotion we step to the gates of heaven with joy and confidence in seeing our beloved (pet name) residing in eternal bliss.

"Blessed be our beloved as the veil is drawn for his/her entrance into heaven."

The cloth or fabric should be folded neatly and placed back upon the altar. A moment of personal reflection on the life shared, the fond memories and precious love should be observed with silence.

The drinking vessels present can be filled with wine, juice or any drink for consumption. All participants gather around your pet, if present, or at the altar. The drinking vessels are held high to honor your deity and your pet, as the participants say:

"Though the loss of our beloved's presence brings sorrow and agony upon our hearts, we know there is not loss, for we shall forever be bound by perfect love. Our separation by physical death is measured by time, and in time we shall be reunited in heaven. Beneath our tearful farewells and aching hearts lies the deepest happiness for our beloved's new life in Spirit. So be it!"

All participants drink deeply. The ritual ends, and may be followed by a feast if desired. Quiet time spent with your pet is ideal as well.

6

Euthanasia: A Personal Decision

ACCEPTING TOTAL RESPONSIBILITY FOR AN ANIMAL COMPANION has its advantages and disadvantages. As painful as it is, there are certain instances in which we must make the final decision for our pet. One such case is euthanasia.

The word euthanasia makes some people cringe, and there are constant debates and arguments between animal lovers and animal rights supporters on the subject. Some see it as unnatural intervention or "playing God," while others see it as necessary and humane relief for a physically suffering, mentally ill or abused animal. The decision to apply or withhold euthanasia is a very personal one, and it is never easy.

Aside from the debates, it is important to consider what the word "humane" truly means. Euthanasia is a legal procedure and a needed option.

Euthanasia is a part of the ultimate responsibility of pet owners who have pledged to support and protect their pets, and to make the best decisions for their pets' well-being and quality of life.

All the pet owners I've known have thought of what they would do if they had to make this decision. Even those who believe that in certain situations euthanasia is the right choice know it is a choice full of responsibility and emotional conflict. We can never make the decision lightly. For our own emotional well-being, we must be certain we are choosing euthanasia as our only recourse, the only way to end our pet's pain and suffering.

When we consider euthanasia, we feel helpless, unable to control the progress of injury or disease. It is common for pet guardians to inflict self-blame when a decision must be made to end a pet's life. You want so much to have your pet with you, yet you realize that, if you choose to put off the decision, your pet may spend further days in physical agony.

My experience with euthanasia is extensive. During my experience in animal rescue, I saw animals who had been so abused that they could not be trained or mentally healed, animals so starved and infested with parasites that there was no hope of recovery. As a foster guardian for strays and unwanted pets, I had to decide many times whether or not to choose euthanasia. In situations where there was no medical hope, the painful choice had to be made. Luckily, these instances were rare.

We are obligated to see that our pets have healthy and comfortable lives. When we are faced with euthanasia as an option, we must feel absolutely right in the decision—for our pets and ourselves. We each have the moral and legal responsibility to make this decision for our pets. Action through love is the best way.

Euthanasia is a delicate issue, and your personal beliefs and spiritual viewpoint will weigh in your decision. Do we have the ethical right to take a life? Pet guardians often value the lives of their pets as they would value a human life—and many people believe it is not right to euthanize humans. Some argue that we are more empowered to prevent suffering in our animals than in our children and ourselves. The law requires us to sustain life in our dying human loved ones who are suffering, yet we may act to end the pain of other living creatures.

Living wills are the closest thing to euthanasia we humans have for ourselves. This will is written prior to, or at the time of, diagnosis of terminal illness, cancer or an accidental, life-threatening injury. I have opted for the living will. I do not want machinery to keep me alive when I can no longer enjoy life or recognize my family and loved ones, or am in constant pain. I would not wish for my family and friends to visit me year after year when I am in this condition. Consider that your pet may feel the same.

Reality and compassion must guide you. You must make the decision on your own—not by doing what others tell you is best— and you will have to live with that decision. No matter what you decide, there will be some people who condemn your decision. You need to be strong. Be guided by your love for your pet.

When making this difficult decision, there are four considerations to keep in mind:

- Euthanasia may be the only way of humanely eliminating the suffering and negative quality of life for your pet.
- No matter what your decision is, you will dwell upon some aspect of it and experience some degree of guilt and self-persecution.
- Your spiritual beliefs regarding our right to make such a life and death decision can assist you, but they can hinder you as well.

- Looking at contemporary social mores regarding birth may help in your decision. Today, test tube babies and artificial insemination are possible, generally accepted and practiced, offering childless couples the great miracle of life and birth. Most people are comfortable with these technologies whereby new life is controlled, and produced, by humankind. Is it wrong that out of love people seek these alternatives when natural conception is not possible? I don't think so. Why then should it be wrong to prompt death through euthanasia as a humane and loving way of ending a suffering life?

When the decision-making process is too much to bear, professional advice from your veterinarian or bereavement counselors may be helpful. You may wish to seek the advice and emotional support of a trusted friend or family member. On the other hand, you may feel that this decision is too personal to share with others, which is fine. The emotional support of family and friends can strengthen your efforts, if needed.

Focus upon your pet's quality of life. Is your pet suffering physical pain? Is he or she mentally ill after eating a poisonous plant or chemical, and unable to live without potentially harming himself or herself, or others? After being diagnosed with cancer or other terminal illness, can your pet live comfortably and free from pain for a few more years? What would be your own wish if you had the same quality of life as your pet?

When I was in junior high school and suffering the hardships of adolescent years—including the awkwardness of being the new kid in school—my family chose a Cocker Spaniel and Poodle mix to join our family. I named her Muley, and she brightened our life. At age eight she began having bladder stones that required a special diet, then surgery. After her first surgery we were relieved that she seemed to be feeling normal again. But shortly thereafter, the stones returned. We were devastated. We continued the special diet, but again she required surgery. After the second surgery, she seemed to lose her zest in life. Not long after that, our veterinarian told us that a third surgery was needed. However, he recommended euthanasia, because he felt that Muley was not strong enough to endure surgery, and believed the vicious, painful cycle would continue.

Heartbroken, we sat down one evening to discuss Muley's quality of life. Finance was not an issue, but her weakened condition and obvious pain were. A couple of days passed of discussion and tearful indecision. Ultimately, it had already been decided in all our hearts. Muley's quality of life was very poor, and to end her suffering, euthanasia was the best choice.

Unfortunately, animals cannot express verbally to us how they feel. In our desire to have our pets remain with us, we often tell ourselves the pet isn't suffering badly, or seems well enough to go on. I went through this delusion with Muley. She appeared in pain, depressed and sad. However, I thought that if we were patient and waited she'd get well.

There is a time when our desires must be logically evaluated. As care providers to our animal companions, we must keep in mind what is best for our pets. Postponing the decision may seem helpful for you, but is it helpful for your pet? Honor your pet's life and your love for your pet by not putting off the procedure when you have established that euthanasia is necessary. Have the procedure done quickly to save your pet additional pain and suffering, and to save yourself the emotional turmoil of delay.

Wrongful Euthanasia

There are situations in which the gift of euthanasia is abused. It is abhorrent, but there are cold-hearted and cruel individuals who view euthanasia as a quick way to dispose of a pet they no longer want. Euthanasia, in this case, is a weapon of selfishness.

When an individual can no longer have a pet, or does not want the pet any longer, then adopting the pet out is an option, or a rescue group can be contacted.

It never ceases to amaze me that people who have the energy to take their pet for euthanasia cannot use that same energy to call an animal rescue group, who will pick up the pet for future adoption.

Sadly, euthanasia receives negative publicity because it has been used as a fast way for people to rid themselves of the burden of locating a new home for their unwanted pet.

The Decision

Your veterinarian will give you a diagnosis and opinion, and explain your options. He or she will offer the truth as medically determined. Your veterinarian may tell you things you don't want to hear, or that will anger you, but remember that he or she has your pet's best interest at heart, and that there is no reason for deception.

In certain instances, your veterinarian, or a dear friend, may suggest that you seek a second opinion. Certainly, this is an option. However, you must realize that when your pet's quality of life deteriorates to the point at which your veterinarian suggests euthanasia, he or she is usually correct in his or her professional opinion.

How do you truly know if euthanasia is the answer? If your beloved pet has been diagnosed with a terminal dysfunction or pain, you owe him or her a dignified and painless end of suffering. Has your veterinarian said that recovery or cure is at all possible? If there is a positive chance, can your pet be kept on medication or somehow pain-free until further diagnosis or treatment can be performed? Are the medical costs excessive and beyond your financial capabilities? Will keeping your pet alive, waiting for further treatment and knowing that he or she is suffering, cause you excessive emotional strain? Only you can answer these questions and make a decision, but placing your confidence in your veterinarian and asking for consultation can help you reach a decision.

In a family, everyone should be made aware of the issue. This includes children. Children should not be made to feel excluded, and their love for the pet should be shown understanding and respect. Protecting your child from the reality of the situation could later result in guilt, anger, a feeling of betrayal and resentment. If you've made the decision, gently speak with your child and ask for input. There should be absolutely no arguing, but soothing explanation and persuasion. Arguing, or displaying a lack of understanding and caring for how your child feels, can leave an emotional scar.

This decision is one that you can never reverse. If you choose euthanasia, you must have confidence in your intuition.

The Euthanasia Procedure

Two different euthanasia procedures are used for pets diagnosed with terminal illness or injury. The veterinarian prepares a syringe containing a massive overdose of a barbiturate and/or sedative. Some veterinarians use two different injections. Once the injection is given, your pet is no longer in pain and suffering, and gently but swiftly slips into sleep and peaceful death.

Euthanasia is not painful for the pet. As the injection is given, one witnesses a beautiful expression of peace and painlessness in the pet's eyes. The pet is soon granted a peaceful death.

You may decide to be present for the administration of the injection. Most pet owners hold and cuddle their beloved pet, watch the pain and suffering disappear and bid a loving farewell. Think how much more comfortable your presence will make your pet. You are your pet's entire life—his or her partner in unconditional love. Though this is not the final moment of your relationship, because your bond will transform into a spiritual one, your presence is the final gesture of love on the physical plane.

Witnessing euthanasia prompts different emotions, some of which can be overwhelming at the time. You may experience sadness in not wanting to let go of the physical bond with your pet. You may feel tremendous happiness in knowing that your pet is now released from physical pain. For everyone, knowing that this is good-bye is emotionally difficult.

Many individuals claim that euthanasia is a spiritual and loving experience. Other individuals say that the experience was very sad, but that there was a feeling of completion and of knowing they had made the right, humane choice.

There is nothing wrong with being unable to be present when euthanasia is administered to your pet. Some people consider the farewell emotionally unbearable. Do not feel you must or should be present. It hurts immensely to cuddle your pet, knowing he or she will no longer be with you in this world.

On a spiritual level, we realize that we have been blessed with the power to act as we deem best concerning our animal companions. Granted the ability to save another living creature from agony, know in your heart that your action shows ultimate love and mercy. Do not allow yourself the torturous feelings of guilt or blame.

Know that most veterinarians are emotionally upset by this procedure as well, even though it is part of their work. Some veterinarians will stay with you after the injection is given, to provide support, while others leave the room to give you privacy. Both actions are gestures of caring, and are done in your best interest. If you prefer your veterinarian to stay, or to give you privacy, you need to specify this beforehand. This will help you and your veterinarian during this emotionally difficult procedure.

There are veterinarians who refuse to allow pet guardians to witness euthanasia. This is due to unpleasant experiences they have had with clients in the past. We can sympathize, because it is common for pet guardians to become emotionally distraught, or otherwise have negative, unexpected responses. An individual may faint or somehow hurt himself or herself in an extreme emotional reaction. A veterinarian is not hiding something by refusing to allow you to be present. Ask your veterinarian if he or she permits witnessing. If not, decide whether you are comfortable with that policy, or consider euthanasia with another veterinarian who allows witnessing.

Euthanasia can be the most distressing decision you will make in life. No one can pass judgment upon you for your choice. It takes the greatest love and devotion, and the most painful courage, to end a suffering life. Your decision should be respected, because it is a painful and difficult one. At this time you need the utmost support, not further emotional stress. It is essential that you remove yourself from the individual who criticizes you, at least for the moment. This is to allow you time to cope, and should not damage or end a valuable relationship.

You should take this moment to seriously think of how you feel regarding euthanasia. It is an issue every pet guardian must face. It is better to be psychologically and emotionally prepared than to make the decision under stress, or through the pressure of others. These negative influences may lead to excruciating regret later.

There are positive aspects to euthanasia. First, you are doing what is best for your beloved pet. Second, in choosing euthanasia, we touch the other side, the darkness of death, and we learn more about our inner selves. You are taking tremendous strides in personal growth by knowing the right choice has been made.

In making your decision, you should not feel you have somehow failed in the care of your pet. You must fight back the guilt, blame and self-defeat and look at yourself as a courageous, compassionate individual, strengthened by the time you have shared with your dear pet. When no other options or hope exist, you've done great service to your pet. Euthanasia can be a great act of love, and now, through your spiritual connection, you and your pet will continue to love each other.

7

Deciding Final Arrangements

ONE OF THE MOST DIFFICULT RESPONSIBILITIES OF PET GUARDIANSHIP is deciding the final arrangements for your pet. If your pet is at the veterinary clinic, and you are too distressed to make a decision yourself, your veterinarian can take care of the arrangements for you. The options available for your pet's final arrangements are many, and in this chapter I explain each so that you can make a rational and suitable decision without future regret.

It is my belief that the more you know about the entire process of final arrangements, the more insightful and rewarding your decision will be. I also believe that final arrangements should be considered before the actual time of death. This pre-planning will not only allow you to grieve without the additional stress of painful decision-making when the tragic time arrives, but will save you from self-recrimination should you make an unconsidered, inappropriate decision at the moment of emotional turmoil.

Should your circumstances force you to make an immediate decision, try to delay it for a few hours. Talk about your options with your veterinarian, or a trusted animal-loving friend, and ask for his or her feelings, knowledge and guidance. If you have already chosen an option that appeals to you, make the arrangements and bring your pet's body to rest right away.

Be certain the final decision is your own—no matter who agrees with your choice or not. You best know your beloved pet and your own feelings and spiritual beliefs. The decision must be made by you, from within your heart and soul.

The Veterinarian Visit

If your pet has been ill and under veterinary supervision; died suddenly from unknown causes, terminal illness or injury; or needed to be euthanized, you will most likely conduct the discussion of death and final arrangements with your veterinarian in his or her office.

You should be aware that in some cases your veterinarian will not explain your options. This is troubling to many pet owners who need this information and support in order to make appropriate arrangements. Often the veterinarian assumes that the pet owner has already considered the available options.

When you take your deceased pet to your veterinary office, the technician or veterinarian will present you with a small form that outlines your options. You must check off the box next to the option you desire, and sign to indicate that your veterinarian has your permission to transport your pet to a pet cemetery or crematorium, or that you prefer to take your pet's body for home burial.

If you are not presented with this form, ask for it. It must be completed, and should be completed by you. Often the veterinarian will complete it out of kindness to save you from additional stress. If you do not choose a final arrangement from the list or specify your wishes, then group cremation will be chosen for you automatically.

Tell your veterinarian what your wishes are and ask for guidance.

Your Pet "On Hold" at the Clinic

When a pet guardian declines to make final arrangements, or delays a decision, the veterinary clinic or shelter will place the pet's body "on hold" within a freezer compartment. The freezer compartment is not available for your examination. You can rest assured that your pet is being handled with respect and treated properly when on hold.

The freezer is usually large, and your pet's body will be carefully placed on a shelf. The freezer will preserve the body until a decision is made. At that point, a truck will arrive from a state-approved cemetery or crematorium to pick up your pet for burial or cremation. In cases where pet guardians do not choose an option, the same truck arrives to pick up the pets for group cremation.

Tags and other identification are carefully filled out and placed upon your pet's body before he or she is admitted into the freezer. There is no need to be concerned that your pet will be "lost" or otherwise misdirected—this is very rare.

Many pet owners cringe in horror at the thought of their beloved pet's body frozen in a dark compartment with other pets. This is a necessary step to preserve the body so that you can take the needed time for your decision. Veterinary clinics, pet cemeteries, crematoriums and other animal-related establishments are equipped by law with freezer compartments. These compartments can be equated to the human morgue at your local hospital. It is illegal in every state for a veterinarian to hold a deceased pet's body without placing it into a freezer until arrangements are made.

You may believe that the freezer compartment must be unpleasant, but that is not so. The freezer is clean and organized. Each pet has his or her own space in which to lie preserved until his or her loving guardian chooses to have the necessary arrangements made.

When your pet is on hold in the freezer and a day has been scheduled for you to come and pick up the body, or other arrangements have been made, your pet will be defrosted in a holding area at room temperature. There is no need for concern that your pet's body will be somehow damaged or mishandled through this process.

If the cemetery or crematorium is picking up your pet, in most cases his or her body will remain frozen and be placed by hand into the freezer compartment on the transport vehicle.

If you are at all concerned that your pet may be lost or not identified, telephone or visit your veterinarian or pet cemetery and request that an employee actually go inside the freezer and check for you. There is absolutely no reason why this cannot be done. Any caring and understanding employee will be more than happy to do so.

Cremation

Group Cremation

Negative feelings about group cremation stem from a lack of education about the process. Group cremation is not unpleasant, as many individuals envision it to be. In fact, it differs from individual cremation only in that more than one animal is cremated at a time. The animals are handled in much the same manner as in individual cremation procedures.

Group cremation is a legitimate option that is often chosen by a veterinary clinic or other animal center that has been instructed by the pet guardian that no other arrangements will be made. Many caring, loving and mourning pet guardians choose group cremation because they simply cannot cope with the emotional distress of viewing their deceased pet. In some cases, the expense of burial or individual cremation is prohibitive.

Group cremation will not be chosen for your pet by veterinary staff without your knowledge. Only at a shelter or clinic where stray animals or abandoned pets are on hold is the choice automatic. There are thousands of stray animals who have no guardian present to make the decision.

Group cremation is a needed and respected option. Contrary to many people's belief, there is nothing disreputable about it. Each state in America has designated, state-approved crematoriums that are carefully inspected; all phases are performed appropriately, and records are carefully kept.

If you choose group cremation for your pet, your veterinarian will notify a crematorium. Your pet will be on hold at your veterinary clinic until picked up by the crematorium's freezer truck or van on the next scheduled pick-up day. Careful records are kept identifying your pet.

The state-approved agency will pick up your pet and others, and place them in the transportation freezer. From the time of pick-up, other scheduled stops are made, and eventually the transportation vehicle will return to the crematorium facility. The driver is met by other employees, who take the deceased pets from the vehicle and record their identities and the location where each was picked up. The pets are then placed on a clean platform where they await group cremation inside the facility.

Group cremation is exactly as the term suggests. The pets are placed side by side in enormous fireproof trays and then slid into large crematorium ovens. The cremation is performed, and, depending upon your state's regulations, the ashes will either be scattered at the crematorium's property or loaded onto another truck to be taken to a landfill. You can telephone your veterinarian to ask about your state's regulations.

The two differences between group cremation and individual cremation are:

- In group cremation, your pet will share his or her tray with other pets.
- You will be unable to receive your pet's ashes in group cremation.

If you wish to avoid group cremation for your pet, you must begin to consider your options and discuss your choice with your veterinarian, or locate a respectable pet cemetery or crematorium now.

If you are uncomfortable with the idea of group cremation, your feelings are another good reason to spay or neuter your pet while he or she is living, so that his or her offspring will not end up among the thousands of strays that sooner or later are group-cremated.

Individual Cremation

Many pet owners desire cremation, but worry that their pet may accidentally, or purposely, be cremated with other pets. This fear comes from hearing or reading about crematoriums run by greedy, unscrupulous individuals. Luckily, such occurrences are rare, and there are things you can do to ensure that your chosen crematorium is reputable.

The wisest advice I can offer you is to ask your veterinarian for a referral, contact and visit various crematoriums and contact state agencies, or the Better Business Bureau, to find out whether a particular crematorium has ever been fined or otherwise accused of malpractice. When contacting a crematorium, ask for references (pet owners who have used their services in the past). Visit a crematorium and ask to be shown around and informed of its services.

If your pet is being held at your veterinary clinic, you must tell your veterinarian that you desire this option. He or she will take care of notifying the establishment you choose, or the crematorium the clinic uses, and arrange for your pet's transportation. You may be given the establishment's telephone number so that you can call and make the arrangements with an employee. Sometimes the veterinarian will provide the establishment with your telephone number and someone will call you to discuss the process. Your veterinarian can also act as your intermediary and handle the entire arrangement if you desire.

If your pet died at home, you can take your pet to be placed on hold at your nearest veterinary clinic and telephone the pet cemetery or crematorium yourself to make arrangements. You may also have the crematorium pick up your pet directly from your home, or you may transport your pet personally to their facility and make the appropriate arrangements in person.

Some veterinary clinics, humane societies and pet cemeteries operate their own crematoriums. You need to telephone such places to find the crematorium closest to you. It is important that you ask for references and ensure that the establishment is respectable.

Your pet's weight and size determine individual cremation fees. Each crematorium has a different fee and deciding factors. Cremation is less expensive than burial in a pet cemetery.

Some crematoriums allow "witnessing." Witnessing is being able to spend a private moment with your pet before cremation, remaining in the facility during the cremation, and not leaving until your pet's ashes are hand-delivered to you. There is normally a fee for this security, but it is well worth it if you are worried about the procedure. The employees will explain the entire operation to you, and they should be very accommodating. The additional cost is due to time set aside for you and your pet exclusively, and to conduct the cremation at your convenience.

Numerous people have asked me, "If I do not witness the cremation, could they lose my pet, or give me the wrong ashes?" You will feel most comfortable if you research the pet cemeteries and crematoriums that you are considering for your pet's final arrangements. It probably will make no difference whether you are present or not—the procedure is the same regardless. Do not feel you must, or even should, be there. Cremation is a lengthy process, and is emotionally stressful.

Individual cremation is conducted by placing your pet's body upon his or her personal tray before introduction into the crematorium oven. The operators of the furnaces keep detailed records of where each pet is placed to ensure that the ashes you receive are definitely your pet's.

The cremation itself takes approximately forty-five minutes. The oven produces heat that burns white-hot. There are not the fiery flames that many associate with cremation; the ovens operate at a much hotter temperature, and the result is "white heat." After the cremation, your pet is removed. Upon the tray rests his or her skeleton.

It is a myth that the extreme heat from the cremation causes the body to suddenly ignite and burst, leaving only ashes behind. The cremation itself does not produce ashes. What results is the skeleton, even if not perfectly intact.

After witnessing many cremations personally, I have learned that a pet's skeleton can sometimes provide clues to an unknown cause of death. Green portions, for example, can be evidence of cancer—the green showing where the cancer attacked. If you find that some of your pet's ashes are another color than white, there may be some similar reason.

Although this fact may be uncomfortable to consider, the ashes of both animals and people are produced using grinding machinery that is meticulously cleaned after each individual use. The individual pet's tray is labeled accordingly, and travels to the machinery that will break down the skeleton into ashes. This is the final step, and it is conducted with care and respect.

In addition to constructing a memorial in your home, you may also wish to memorialize your pet by storing his or her ashes in a special repository called a columbarium in a pet cemetery. You may wish to find out which of your local pet cemeteries offer this service. You'll learn more about pet cemeteries in the next section.

Burial

There are several burial options you can consider. Many individuals choose burial for the peace of mind they feel in knowing that their beloved pet is resting within Mother Earth, and that the burial site can be memorialized and visited. Interment has been practiced since the beginning of history, and it is probable that it existed even earlier in humanity. Many graphic records exist from classical Egyptian times of hieroglyphic writing containing images of mummified dogs and cats.[1]

Pet cemeteries exist worldwide, but the majority reside within the United States. Most are beautifully landscaped, spacious and well cared for. Many cemeteries have special provisions made against the land ever being sold or used for any other purpose. You can ask your pet cemetery to provide you with a copy of the legal papers that contain these provisions.

The expense for burial through a pet cemetery varies. Usually the cost begins at a couple of hundred dollars and increases depending upon what burial plot is selected, what type of casket is desired, the type of grave marker chosen, and more.

Many humane societies and pet cemeteries offer community burial as a less expensive option. This is not the "mass grave" that many fear. When done suitably, the community burial allows your pet to be buried in his or her own spot of earth, without a casket. This is very much like a home burial in which the pet is laid to rest simply within the womb of Mother Earth. The community burial is not expensive and indeed preserves your pet's memory with dignity. Your veterinarian or SPCA office can direct you regarding this type of burial arrangement.

How to Arrange a Burial

For a more formal burial at a pet cemetery, it is wise to pre-plan and visit several cemeteries in your geographical area to find one to your liking. As stressed previously, you should acquire references and check with the town hall or Better Business Bureau to ensure that no complaints have ever been made regarding the facility.

How do you know if the cemetery is reputable or not? This question can only be answered by suggesting that you visit each individual cemetery and do some detective work to provide you with peace of mind. In fact, making it a point to talk face-to-face with the cemetery's owner can tell you much.

There are pet cemeteries that have existed for almost a century, providing excellent service. Most facility owners and staff are eager to prove they are reputable and offer you a dignified final resting place for your pet. As with preparation for human death, it is wise to pre-plan and investigate cemeteries beforehand, while your beloved family member is still living.

When visiting a pet cemetery or crematorium, take along family members or someone close to you. Another person can help by offering his or her opinions, likes and dislikes, and may have questions or concerns that you have not thought of. The staff at the facility should be friendly and eager to offer proof of their reputation and legitimacy, and also to explain every detail of how a burial plot, casket and grave marker are chosen. The staff can also explain the contract for burial.

Every pet cemetery has a contract. Read it carefully. Ask to examine one in advance. Many contracts state that after your death, your pet's burial site can be re-used. In some cases, when a payment plan is drawn up, the contract may state that if a payment has not been made by a certain time your pet's body can be exhumed and disposed of by the facility in order to re-sell the plot to someone else. A pet cemetery is a business and, like other businesses, may repossess an item if the agreed-upon payments are not made. You should not allow these potential facts to scare you, but you must note every detail of the contract before proceeding.

Request a tour of the cemetery grounds. Look around carefully—are the grounds beautifully kept? Examine burial markers and sites—are the grave markers kept in good condition? Have weeds and grass been allowed to overgrow markers, or are they kept cut back properly? The employee who guides you on the tour should be willing to explain every detail of the cemetery. Ask any question. The only stupid questions are those not asked. Have the friend or family member accompanying you ask questions as well, and express his or her opinions to you.

Inside the facility or cemetery office, you should ask to be shown grave markers, caskets and other items pertaining to your pet's burial. Do not allow yourself to be sold on expensive items if you find an inexpensive one that is suitable. Remember, as much as a respectable cemetery or crematory cares, sales is part of their job. Do not allow yourself to be manipulated into purchasing items you do not need or desire.

If your pet is on hold in the facility's freezer compartment, you can ask to view it, but do not become angered if your request is denied. Usually this is done for your sake; viewing frozen pets upon shelves is not pleasant for anyone, and the employee will be concerned that you will become upset. There is no real need to view this compartment. There is nothing hidden or negative about it. This compartment serves the positive preservation of your pet and is a necessary step, no matter how you feel about the idea.

Whether you are pre-planning or dealing with a recent death, you will be shown photographs and actual items, such as burial plots and markers, to choose from. To choose a burial plot you will tour the cemetery with an employee and decide from those available. Some plots cost more than others. A "lawn plot" may be inexpensive compared to a plot within a grove of pine trees. If your family is present, allow your children and other members to comment on their likes and dislikes. Sometimes you may wish to purchase the burial plot in advance but prefer to wait to choose a casket or grave marker. This is usually fine; those items can be paid for and added to the contract at a later time.

Wooden caskets cost more than plastic caskets. In some cases, you may choose the lining of the casket, which may be satin, cotton or some other material.

Grave markers can be ordered in brass or granite, in a variety of sizes and shapes, with your choice of inscription. The employee will provide you with an estimated total cost of the items you have chosen.

Before signing any document or contract, read it thoroughly. If some part of it troubles you, ask that it be explained in detail. If you do not understand why a certain policy exists, ask. After you sign the contract and payment is made, your pet's final arrangements are complete.

The Burial

Depending upon what cemetery and burial options you choose, each burial will be unique and different. Usually a date is scheduled at the signing of the contract if your pet is deceased. If the plot is purchased in advance, the burial date will obviously be scheduled later, at the time of death. Usually the pet cemetery has set aside hours when wakes, funeral proceedings and burials take place. At times the cemetery may make exceptions to their schedule policy if absolutely necessary for your convenience; however, some will not. Many offer weekend burials, usually on Saturday.

On the day of your pet's burial, there is much preparation at the pet cemetery in addition to your own preparation of dressing your children, planning a ritual for the wake or proceedings and preparing yourself emotionally. The cemetery takes your pet off hold and allows him or her to resume his or her natural state, no longer frozen. Your pet's body is carefully and kindly groomed, just as it would be at any pet grooming shop. Your pet is bathed and his or her nails may be clipped. Special consideration is given in brushing and drying your pet's fur so that it is pleasantly styled and perfumed. Rest assured that your pet is handled with care and respect. Often the groomer is very meticulous and careful, because he or she wants you to be pleased with your pet's appearance—to feel that your pet appears as most fondly remembered.

Often before you arrive your pet is gently laid in his or her casket. If there is a blanket with the casket liner, it is often pulled up to your pet's shoulders, symbolizing peaceful rest. Your pet's head is normally laid on one side to appear as if he or she is sleeping in a soft and sacred bed. You may ask for your pet to be laid in another position at the time of scheduling the burial, if you prefer. Some pet guardians wish to see their pets laid out as if sleeping on the family couch.

Your pet's casket is placed in a viewing room, sometimes behind folded doors that divide the casket viewing area from the rest of the room. When you arrive, the doors will be opened.

Once you arrive, an employee, usually the person you made arrangements with initially, greets you and helps to prepare you. Last-minute questions and concerns are discussed. He or she may then open the folding doors, or open the casket for your viewing.

Then the employee exits until you call him or her when finished viewing, or in need. At this viewing time you may conduct a ritual or simply view your beloved pet with family or friends, and give him or her a loving farewell.

After the viewing, you will summon the employee if he or she has not arranged with you to arrive at a specific time. Your pet's casket is then closed and sealed before you. This ritual of sealing the casket allows you to witness that your pet is forever sealed within and will not be disturbed. It is done to give you peace of mind.

The employees will then take your pet to a vehicle, sometimes a cemetery truck, and drive him or her to the burial site. You can ask to walk to the site with the employee who has assisted you, or you can walk alone or drive. Do not be afraid to ask the person who has guided you through the burial process to ride or walk with you if you would like him or her to be with you. These employees are present to give you sincere support and guidance, and it is no imposition to ask that they accompany you.

At the burial site you will find an opening, normally six to eight feet into the earth. The opening was made that morning by cemetery employees. You will be able to stand directly at the burial site as your pet, sealed in the casket, is lowered into it carefully with ties or bands of sturdy nylon. Afterward, you may ask for a moment to say a prayer for your pet or a short, last-minute ritual. Many individuals bring rose petals to toss upon the casket as a symbol of their everlasting love. Next, the employees will begin to cover your pet's casket with earth, usually by hand with a shovel. It is traditional for the pet guardian to be offered the first toss of earth into the burial site. Once the site is filled with earth, an instrument that looks like a pillar with a square base is used to forcefully pack the soil. The green grass, in the shape of a cut square, like a cutting of sod, is placed atop the soil and packed down. Once the burial of your pet is completed, a grave marker may be immediately installed, or arrangements can be made to purchase one and have it installed later.

You are then free to remain at your pet's burial site as long as needed. You may visit any time, adhering to cemetery hours. Flowers, wreaths, religious articles and holiday decorations are usually permitted. Your pet is laid to rest with dignity, and crosses the threshold to exist upon the spiritual plane in peace.

Home Burial

Informal backyard burial is a common choice for pet owners who own land, or have family, friends or a neighbor with land. Your decision to conduct home burial must take into consideration the availability of land and local laws governing burial in undesignated places.

Burying your pet on your own land is extremely satisfying. You conduct every aspect of your pet's burial. Home burial is thought of as returning a loved animal companion to nature. There is no need for extravagance—wrapping your pet in a favorite blanket or one of your sweaters, and laying him or her to rest with some cherished belongings and toys, is a beautiful, loving ritual in itself.

Informal burial requires your attention to practical matters. Even if the land chosen is your property, home burial may be against the law in your area. Your first step is to check with your local government offices, such as the municipal court clerk, city clerk, or police department. Find out whether or not home burial is permitted in your locality. A special permit may be required. There may be certain regulations, such as that the grave must be a minimum of four feet deep.

The legalities exist because local officials are unable to establish control over the depth and number of informal burial plots. This is dangerous because, if a grave is too shallow, the decomposed remains could be uncovered by children or animals, causing a potential health hazard.

Taking proper steps to determine your legal rights is a must. It is heartbreaking to be told that your pet needs to be moved, and to be required to pay fines and attend legal proceedings, while you are in the depths of your grief.

Home burial is simple, inexpensive and satisfying, but does not guarantee a permanent, final resting place for your pet. The land may be sold in the future and used for a different purpose. A new owner may decide to build upon the land or otherwise unearth your pet's grave.

If your pet dies in the winter, the ground is often frozen. Informal burial is impossible, and your pet will need to be placed on hold with your veterinarian or local animal shelter until the ground thaws. The waiting period can be long and, for some pet guardians, too emotionally stressful.

If home burial is your choice, I suggest calling your veterinarian, or a reputable pet cemetery, to ask how the burial may be properly done. If placing your pet directly into the earth makes you uncomfortable, pet cemeteries and related mail order companies offer a variety of caskets you can choose for home use.

Again, the depth at which you bury your pet is important. Local town officials and your veterinarian should be able to provide a suitable recommendation.

City dwellers and renters often would like the option of informal burial, but have no access to available land. I do not recommend burial in city parks unless permission is granted from the court clerk or appropriate city office. Renters, even in rural areas, must also take necessary steps to acquire permission from the property owner and local government offices.

While this practice is rather uncommon, it is sometimes possible to bury your pet in the country, or on state farmlands. Farmers and landowners will grant permission on occasion. Introduce yourself, explain your situation to them, and ask.

After home burial, you can decorate your pet's site however you wish. A friend of mine in New Jersey placed a stone circle around her dog's burial site and planted beautiful perennial flowers within it. Perennial flowers are symbolic of the cycle of birth, death and rebirth. She also planted a flower garden on one side and a vegetable garden on the other. Wind chimes and decorations beautify her pet's burial site. When there is no wind, but the wind chimes play, she says it is her dog's spirit greeting her.

It can be most comforting to have your pet at home, where you can visit him or her in the body, and in the spirit, whenever desired.

Other Options

Other options exist that are costly but deserve mention here. They are not available at every cemetery or crematorium, but the toll-free number I provide at the end of this chapter will help you find the closest facility to your geographical location.

Freeze-Drying

Freeze-drying should not be confused with your pet being on hold. Freeze-drying is a lengthy and expensive procedure in which your pet is placed into any position you desire—sitting, lying down—and any facial expression you desire—mouth open, mouth shut, eyes looking straight ahead etc. This is done by specialists at the facility, who position your pet using an intricate holding device. You should be aware that your pet's natural eyes will be removed and false eyes given. Your pet will be groomed, positioned and placed within an enormous freeze-drying tank, perhaps with other pets. The process can take months to over a year to complete. By freeze-drying internally, so that only your pet's "bodily shell" remains, the process preserves your pet's fur, skeleton, and appearance forever. The cost is usually over a thousand dollars. The size of your pet, type of pet, desired position and other factors affect the cost.

Once the process is completed, your pet is removed from his or her supporting structure and has permanently been freeze-dried into position. You are telephoned or contacted by mail to let you know that the process is complete and you can pick up your pet.

Many individuals then place their pet in a favorite resting area in the home. At times a sanctuary is designed in the home, where the pet can rest forever.

Taxidermy

Like freeze-drying, though usually less expensive, taxidermy allows you to preserve your pet's external form. The body will be artistically prepared, stuffed and positioned as desired.

Taxidermists also may be consulted regarding other forms of preservation of your pet. Some pet owners wish to keep their pet's pelt to frame or rest on a living room furnishing, or to cuddle when reminiscing. A taxidermist can provide you with many options for preserving all or a portion, such as the fur, of your pet. Usually taxidermists can be found in any geographical location where deer hunting and other forms of hunting are done. Check your Yellow Pages for a listing.

I have attempted to offer you the most detailed information about final arrangements for your pet so that you can plan with a good understanding of the proceedings. Very often, pet owners are so emotionally distressed and devastated that they are unable to understand what is involved in making final arrangements, and how the different procedures are conducted. Confusion leads to more frustration and hurt, as pet owners feel guilty that they are making arrangements they know little about.

To find cemeteries or crematoriums that perform any of the procedures described above, you can look in your telephone book's Yellow Pages or ask your veterinarian. If you live somewhere that does not have these facilities readily available, you may contact the organization below by mail or phone. The information is free.

International Association of Pet Cemeteries
Stephen Drown
P.O. Box 163, 5055 Route 11
Ellenburg Depot, NY 12935
Phone: (518) 594-3000
Fax: (518) 594-8801
Website: www.iaopc.com

Make the choice for your pet's final resting place from your heart. Do not concern yourself with the opinions of those who are insensitive or unsympathetic. Be pleased in knowing that your choice is for the best and expresses the undying love between yourself and your pet. The decision is an intimate one that can only be made by you with love.

8

Other Forms of Pet Loss

PET LOSS EXTENDS BEYOND THE SEPARATION INEVITABLE THROUGH physical death. There are instances in life, some unavoidable, when your pet has run away from home, or needs a new home. These situations cause a very real and similar grief to that experienced in the physical death of a pet.

The difference between bereavement caused by physical separation and that caused by physical death is that in separation you know that your pet continues to live without you. This type of grief includes anxiety about your pet's happiness and safety in a new environment, and acceptance of your pet's new life.

Pet lovers are devastated when a situation arises in which a beloved pet must be given away. Many pet guardians think of their pets as surrogate children. Every available option is examined and tried. Sadly, on rare occasions there are simply no options.

In this chapter we will discuss the difficult decision of giving up a beloved pet to a new home, and the trauma of a runaway pet. There is a very real grief and emotional upset in both situations that need our recognition and proper care.

Giving Up Your Pet

As much as every pet lover dreads it, there are situations in which a pet can no longer remain in the family. In most cases, the cause is a child's allergy to pet dander. Other reasons include a job transfer, moving to a new residence where pets are not allowed, a special medical need the pet has developed that cannot be sufficiently fulfilled, or a divorce. Each of these reasons is valid and real. Circumstances may arise in which our devotion and love for our pet cannot overcome the obstacle of change in our lives. Below I'll address several situations that pose a risk to pet ownership, and mention viable options for each.

Allergic Reaction

If your child has an allergy, viable options include speaking with your family physician about medication that can control the allergic reaction, or confining your pet to a certain area of your home to decrease the dander. An allergic reaction can be serious. Respiratory problems and related symptoms can be disabling. Have your child examined by an allergist. The allergist can assess the matter and suggest a course of action.

Reducing the amount of fabric in your home, ridding your home of carpeting, using blinds instead of curtains, or housing your pet outside may be helpful. This last option, or confining your pet to an area of your home, is acceptable if your pet's quality of life is not adversely affected.

Sometimes allergy shots and other measures fail, and the only solution is finding your pet a new home. This can be emotionally overwhelming for you and your child. Frequently, a child will resent his or her own body as the agent of this unwelcome change. In making any decision, your child's quality of life, and that of your pet, must be carefully considered.

Relocation

When faced with a job transfer and relocation to a new residence where pets are not allowed, your options are limited. You could remain in the employment and residence already held, but sacrificing the new employment and its needed benefits may not be an option. Often, the awaiting job offers financial rewards and medical benefits that your family desperately needs. Your only option might be to search for another job.

If the new employer is paying for your family move and has chosen the new residence, which is a common practice in corporations, you can request a move to a residence allowing pets.

The bottom line is that you need to assess whether the new job transfer is an important step for you and your family, what options are available to you regarding your pet and, should all other options fail, whether your family will be capable of accepting that your pet needs a new home.

Rental Housing

Individuals who rent find that there are a limited number of landlords willing to allow pets. You may find that, while a previous landlord allowed pets, now every landlord approached in your search for a new residence refuses. If at all possible, try to remain in the current rental dwelling and search for another landlord who allows pets. Placing a personal ad in the newspaper to advertise your need for a rental that allows pets is one idea. Moving to a suitable residence and keeping your pet is the best option, though sometimes this is easier said than done. If buying a house or a mobile home is impossible, or if an immediate move is necessary, you unfortunately have limited choices.

Tenants who do not have a signed lease can find themselves evicted or issued with a court notice for having a pet. There may in fact have been a verbal agreement, but unless the landlord specifies in writing that pets are allowed on the premises, tenants are at risk. If a tenant cannot solve the issue with the landlord and keep the pet, loses a court case or cannot afford the cost of a lawsuit, there are only two options: attempt to relocate or place the pet for adoption.

A New Marriage

If you are a pet guardian in a new marriage and find that your loving spouse is unable to tolerate your pet, try to uncover the reason and find a positive solution. The reason may be a phobia or a general dislike. Options exist, such as having your pet live outdoors or confined to a certain area of your living space—as long as your pet will still enjoy a positive quality of life.

Often this situation can become very stressful. The new marriage and the love for the pet are weighed. It is not uncommon for the marriage to be preserved and, sadly, the pet adopted out to a new home.

A New Baby

A childless couple who has lived with a pet for years may find that once their newborn baby is brought home, there are risks to the child. Frequently, the pet in this situation is a large dog.

Pets rarely pose a risk to children. However, a pet who is not obedience trained, or has a history of destructive tendencies, may be a concern. Your options are taking your pet to obedience classes, discussing the situation with your veterinarian, or possibly creating a schedule whereby your pet and new baby do not come in contact with each other until your child is older—such as allowing your pet the run of the house only when your child sleeps.

Hours of Employment

It is not uncommon for a job promotion, new work hours or required travel to create a problem in your pet's care and quality of life. If there is no one to help care for your pet while you are working or traveling, consideration for your pet's quality of life is a must. You need to consider searching for new employment, hiring a pet sitter or, if these are impossible, placing your pet for adoption.

Financial Problems

Corporate downsizing, unemployment and financial hardship are realities of today's society. Financial instability can jeopardize your ability to care for your pet. The cost of food, medical care and other pet-related necessities can be a problem.

Aging people on fixed incomes are often unable to support themselves and their pet.

If you are suddenly met with financial hardship and are unable to take advantage of the options listed in this chapter, finding your pet a new home, for the well-being of your family and your pet, may be a necessity.

The Elderly

The financial restraints and health problems of the elderly can affect their ability to care for their pets. Frequently, elderly individuals must move to an apartment complex for the aged, where pets are not allowed. Unfortunately, many are unaware of state or city laws that might allow them to keep their animal companions in rental situations, or do not know how to exercise their rights under these laws. Local animal advocates, humane societies or elder care agencies can help.

A pet can literally be your only source of companionship. Providing care and love for your pet can sustain your health, sense of well-being and vitality. Ask your family members or someone you can trust to assist you and to help you search for options. If your separation from your beloved pet is inevitable, enjoy your remaining time with your pet and, with the help of a trusted friend or relative, see that he or she is given to a good home.

When a New Home is Needed

If you need to find your pet a new home, realize that your love for your pet is not in question. You may think you will be condemned by other animal lovers for making the necessary decision of giving away your cherished and precious companion. Recognize this feeling and assumption as a cruel symptom of your grief: guilt. Do not emotionally batter yourself.

Whatever your situation is, you need to accept it, enjoy the remaining time with your pet, and cope. There is no reason for you to place yourself on trial in your mind. Once you have taken ample time to evaluate your options and have found that giving your pet away is necessary, then you must accept the reality and begin your search for a suitable new home.

If you have a family, it is very important that the situation and the decision-making process be explained and open for discussion with the entire family. Your children must be informed so that they fully understand the circumstances and can get a positive start in coping with their grief. Children need to feel included in each delicate step.

Children often consider their pet as a best friend or a sibling, with whom they share all the joys and pains of life. In this type of relationship between child and pet, a child may have real concerns that he or she will be given up as well. It may seem illogical to adults that such a questions would come to mind, but care must be taken not to laugh off such an inquiry. Explain the circumstances to your child and let him or her know why such fears will never be realized.

Prepare for your child's reaction. Your child will be full of heartache, shock and denial, and will wonder why his or her beloved pet must go. Explaining adult decisions to children is never easy, but pre-planning can help a great deal. Each question or protest from your child should be recognized and dealt with, not discounted. Having to give away a precious friend will be an overwhelming loss for your child. Provide comforting talk and reassurance, and involve your child at every step of the way. With positive guidance and understanding, you equip your child with mental tools to cope in a healthy manner.

How to Cope

After your family has come to terms with the situation, it is important that the remaining time spent with the pet be enjoyed. Your child may wish to spend every free moment with the pet; this is fine and should not be discouraged.

Separation from your pet when circumstances demand it causes guilt, disbelief and denial. You need to give proper attention to your child's grieving as well as your own, and to allow him or her the freedom to speak his or her feelings.

Guilt is an emotion we inflict upon ourselves relentlessly and wrongfully. When you have done all you can and tried your best to find some way to keep your pet, you must allow your mind peace from self-reprimand. If an effort is made to take the energy concentrated in guilt and focus it upon acquiring a safe, secure and happy new home for your pet, you will feel much better in knowing that you've done all you can for your pet in your last days together.

Your pet can sense your feelings and emotions. He or she knows when something is wrong with you, or when you are deeply upset. When painful and negative emotions surface, they can stress your pet. Try to enjoy your remaining time together, and project positive energies to make the situation comfortable for you both. Later, when you reflect on this time, you will have the peace of mind of knowing that your last days together were happy ones.

Hidden in your deep love for your pet is the notion that only you can best provide for him or her. We pride ourselves on being animal lovers and care providers. It is unwise, however, to assume that no other human being can provide as we do. If your pet is healthy and can be placed into a new home, there is every reason that this should be done.

There are people who, when faced with giving up their pet, choose to have the healthy pet euthanasized, assuming that no one else could possibly provide the care and love the pet needs. This is a selfish thought. Euthanasia is not ethical unless your pet is unhealthy or incapable of functioning around other people. You should opt for a pet adoption. There is no reason to rob your pet of the opportunity to experience love and happiness in a new environment.

Your worries about whether or not your pet can cope with the change and find happiness in a new life are typical, as are concerns that that new life be free from abuse and neglect. I hope the section below, which examines how best to find your pet a suitable home, will lessen your worries.

Using an Organization to Find a Good Home

You will have many concerns about your pet's new life and environment. These concerns should be outlined on paper by you, and all family members, to be presented to the person to whom you are giving your pet—whether a new guardian or an animal rescue group. Voicing your concerns and desires does make a difference and can ease the process.

There are many ways to go about locating a new home. If searching for a new home yourself is too painful, you can contact a pet rescue or adoption organization—one that does not apply euthanasia to those pets not adopted in a specific period of time. You need to ask any adoption service if they have this policy.

Pet adoption organizations can ease the stress and emotional pain of taking part in your pet's transition to a new home. There are individuals who dearly love their pet but cannot emotionally handle the home-hunting process. Nonprofit organizations that provide foster homes are the best choice. Having volunteered for one myself, I can say that volunteers take the utmost care in interviewing potential new guardians and providing a comfortable environment for your pet in the process. Foster homes are loving families who provide care and a home environment, like the one your pet has been accustomed to with you. Many times, foster families will adopt a pet in their care—another positive consideration.

Your local telephone book, or your veterinarian, local pound or state kennel club, usually has a list of local organizations. It is best to call each one, present your questions and concerns, and continue searching until you find a group that is satisfactory. You can even ask a member of the group to visit your home, or to meet with you and your pet somewhere. This will provide an opportunity for you to settle any questions or concerns you may have about the group, its activities and what will happen to your pet.

Aside from rescue and adoption groups, you can place an ad in your local paper and interview potential homes yourself. Personal ads of this sort are not costly, and the response is usually great. Out of all the responses there is a good chance that many will be suitable homes. In choosing this method, you have complete control of where your pet will start a new life. This requires scheduling interviews and welcoming strangers into your home. If you live alone, it is best to have a friend or relative with you when people arrive.

Interviewing Potential Guardians

Ask necessary questions. Does the family have other pets? If so, can they bring their pets to your home to interact with yours? I remember a couple who came to our home in response to an ad for a foster dog we had, a Rottweiler named Duke. I suggested they bring their eight-year-old dog with them, which they did. The two dogs did not get along. The meeting certainly saved the dogs, them and us from the possible trouble that could have occurred had the family adopted Duke.

Ask if the prospective guardian has children. Children should accompany parents to your home. If the child dislikes or mistreats your pet, you will be present to witness it. The child's reaction and behavior will help you decide if the home is suitable.

Ask potential guardians if they rent or own their home. If a family rents, you need to require a signed notice from the landlord stating that your pet will be allowed to live on the premises. From my experience in the pet adoption league, you may find people who rent, adopt your pet and later are told by a landlord to get rid of the pet. The new guardians may not inform you. Usually, the pet is then taken to a pound, put out on the street or given away. A family that tells you their rental home allows pets needs to provide proof.

What outdoor activities will your pet, especially a dog, have with this family? Does the property have a fenced-in yard, a kennel or a tie-out leash, or does the property sit upon a busy highway? Find out and take all answers into consideration.

What hours do the parents work? Never accept the answer that a child will care for the pet. Children may desire pets, but we know that actual care for the pet is usually the parents' responsibility. If both parents work ten-hour days and are rarely home, you need to take that into consideration.

All of these questions are typical of adoption service groups. Such groups are very strict in interviewing, and reject possible homes more often than they accept them. You must use the same caution. Do not feel uncomfortable with interrogating people. People who sincerely wish to adopt your pet will be open and understanding of your concerns. Anyone who refuses to answer or provide essential proof, such as a landlord's permission, can be rejected.

During an interview, if you sense that the prospective guardian is unsuitable, thank him or her for his or her interest and state that another family is being considered. You can add that if the family decides against the adoption, you will be in touch. Any rejection should be polite.

Once you have chosen a home, record the new family's physical address (not just a mailing address), and telephone number. After a couple of days, you and a friend can drive past the new family's home. If it appears that the people have lied—they live in an apartment complex instead of a private home, for example—or if anything looks undesirable or suspicious, have the courage to stop and confront the new guardian. Do not jump to conclusions—there may be a misunderstanding. Discuss the problem with them on a positive note, and negotiate a solution.

Your veterinarian has clients that have used his or her services for years. Ask your veterinarian if he or she can recommend a new home or advise other clients that your pet is available for adoption. Another client of your veterinarian is ideal. Visiting the veterinarian regularly clearly demonstrates that the individual is a good care provider.

There are families who house their pets in a commercial kennel when in-house living arrangements are unavailable, or when providing sufficient care, perhaps because of work hours, is a problem. Kennel boarding is an option rarely chosen because of the expense and the discomfort for the pet.

It is important that all issues, concerns and desires be voiced and discussed within your family. Whatever option is chosen must be agreed upon as the best, and be properly acted upon. If the option feels comfortable and secure for you and your pet, then it is the correct one. Remember, only you and your family can determine what is best for your pet.

The mere thought of giving away a pet is troubling to us all. A fellow pet lover who condemns you is sharing in your frustration and pain without knowing all the details of the situation.

Celebrate the love you share with your pet, and make your last moments together positive. Enjoy your time with your pet, and experience every moment to the fullest.

Saying Good-Bye

When the moment arrives to say good-bye, there will be tears and deep sorrow. Be certain to begin saying farewell before the new guardian, or the pet adoption volunteer, arrives. When other people are present, we tend to clam up, missing the chance to express ourselves they way we'd like to. Remember, whoever comes to your home for your pet realizes the agony you feel. Taking away a precious part of someone's life is painful in itself. When the new guardian is present, try not to prolong the farewell more than necessary. It is common for both the new guardian and the grieving guardian to show sadness. While this is fine, you do not want to stress your pet or the new guardian. They both have much excitement and change to deal with in becoming acquainted.

Runaway and Stolen Pets

During my involvement with the Pet Adoption League, my husband and I fostered an eleven-year-old Schnauzer. The dog had been picked up by a pound in an urban area, and later was taken from the pound by a group volunteer.

The Schnauzer stayed with us for about two weeks. He became "one of the family" in our home. Because of his age, temperament and nature, I was certain he was lost and from a good home.

After his second week with us, I received a phone call. Our adoption league had placed an ad in the local newspaper of the area where the dog had been found, and received a response. The dog's family lived miles away from where he had been found—he must have wandered far, trying to get home.

That evening, the family arrived at our home. Once I opened the front door and invited the people inside, the little gray Schnauzer leaped upon them in glee. The family was reunited in tears and great joy—and excited barks! I stood tearful—witnessing a reunion that easily could never have happened.

The most important part of this story is how the dog became lost. On Thanksgiving Day, the family had relatives over for dinner. The front door was open more frequently, and for longer periods, than usual. The dog was always leash walked and was never allowed outdoors alone. When the opportunity arose, he decided to stroll out the door, unnoticed in the swarm of visiting relatives.

We can understand how easily a dog could exit a busy household unnoticed. It was very painful for the family to discovering the mishap that had caused their pet's disappearance.

A dog may run away when his or her outdoor tie-out breaks, or may escape from an outdoor kennel. A cat may waltz out a door accidentally left open, or escape through a broken window screen. The sudden instinct to chase another animal may lead a pet astray. Birds sometimes escape from their cages and leave through an open window or door. All of these situations, and many others, can happen even with most careful consideration.

We berate ourselves for allowing such a terrible thing to happen, forgetting that even the greatest of care and control over our pets is overcome by accidental mishaps. All too easily, we can turn our anger, disbelief and regret inward to punish ourselves, wallowing fruitlessly in guilt.

Reunion with a lost or stolen pet is desperately sought, but rarely possible. Efforts to find your pet must be made, but once you've done everything possible in your search, without result, you need to realize and accept the loss.

Stolen pets are definitely beyond our control. A thief is a calculating individual who stalks victims without their knowing. Usually the perpetrator analyzes your environment and acts only when he or she is certain that no witnesses are present. You are not to blame.

Anger evolves quickly when our lives are suddenly and cruelly changed by another individual. When an intruder decides to come into our lives it is no fault of our own. No matter what protective and careful measures you take daily, or would have taken, the intruder wanted your pet and would have found a way to steal him or her.

There is a sense of violation. It seems inconceivable that another human being would dare destroy the loving relationship between you and your pet. But the person who stole your pet has a different set of values, and lives by selfishness and greed.

Pets are stolen for many reasons. Some perpetrators desire a pedigree pet and cannot afford to pay for one. It is known that certain persons will steal pets to sell to laboratories that use animals in medical research or product testing. Luckily, this incident is becoming less frequent as laboratories replace animal testing with alternatives. There are also cases in which an individual steals a pet merely to collect the reward money from the desperate owner.

Once you realize your pet has run away or been stolen, grief surfaces. You know that your pet is still living, and you worry for his or her well-being. You are desperate to find your pet and save him or her from possible harm. You need to cope with knowing that other individuals may be caring for, or harming, your pet. These possibilities, coupled with bereavement, are nearly unbearable, but have faith: there are actions you can take that may help you trace or recover your pet.

What To Do

Your pet has run away, or has been stolen, and the situation seems unreal. Amidst the shock, disbelief, denial and anger, you are in a panic.

If you have children, tell them what has happened. I recommend that you quickly come to terms with the situation and plan exactly how you will explain it to your family, especially your children. This is difficult. In your own shock and sorrow, you may barely be capable of understanding the circumstances and what should be done.

Gather your family into a comfortable room and inform them. Children are as perceptive as adults in knowing when something is wrong, so you should not attempt to hide the details from your family. You may wish to make an effort to find the pet first and protect your family from distress, but you need to accept that your pet may not be found. Obviously, your children will notice that their pet is missing. Hiding the facts, even with good intentions, can be damaging to your children's trust in you.

Your discussion should be open and honest. When questions arise of how, when and why the pet was lost or taken, you must reveal details that you have and be truthful when you cannot provide answers. Assure your children that although you do not have all the answers, with their help the family will do its best to get those answers and find the pet.

Encourage your children to become involved in the attempt to recover the lost pet. The following actions may help you find answers to your questions and even recover your pet:

1. Place a personal ad in your local newspaper right away. The cost is minimal, and there is a good chance that the ad will reach someone who has at least seen your pet. Many times, someone has seen an animal wandering or walking down a neighborhood street. Thinking that the animal is a neighbor's pet, they will not stop and take him or her home. If you can find out what area your pet has recently frequented, that will assist in tracking and, hopefully, recovering your pet.

2. Design "missing" and "reward" signs that are easily read from a distance. Fluorescent poster board with information written in bold magic marker is ideal for capturing people's attention. Be sure to include your pet's breed, name, age, color of eyes, fur pattern and color(s) and your address and telephone number.

   Place signs upon telephone poles in your neighborhood. Go into local businesses and request that your sign be posted.

Laundromats, grocery stores, libraries, schools, parking lots, restaurants and other public places frequented by people day and night are recommended.

If you offer a reward for information, or for the return of your pet, do not specify an amount of money on the sign. If the reward is attractive, you could receive a number of false calls. Beware of anyone who asks you to forward money by mail, bank transfer or other means in exchange for the safe return of your pet. Unless the person arrives at your home with your pet, do not provide reward money.

When my mother's cat ran away, she designed large, eye-catching signs complete with a photo of her cat. She placed them at her local deli, department stores, grocery stores etc. A couple of weeks later, an individual telephoned her to report seeing her cat killed on a local highway. The caller had seen my mother's sign in a local department store. If she had not posted her "missing" signs, she would never have known.

3. If you believe your pet was stolen, call the police. A police report must be filed in case your pet is found. Filing a police report will enable you to prosecute the thief, which might save other pet owners from suffering the same loss. The police may already have a record of cases in your area, and your notifying them could greatly help your search as well as that of other pet owners. The police will also advise you of local pounds, animal shelters and other establishments you can contact to find out if your pet is being held there.

4. You can conduct an effective search over the telephone. Contact animal shelters and pounds within a twenty-mile

radius around your town; lost pets will sometimes wander and can cover a great distance. Veterinarians, animal control officers, forest rangers in state parks, business owners, neighbors, all pet-related businesses and rescue or adoption organizations should be contacted.

5. Visit local pounds and animal shelters with a photo of your pet. Volunteers and employees who work different shifts will be able to refer to the photo should a new animal arrive.

Each animal shelter, pound or pet-related business you visit or telephone will provide you with more places to contact. Each contact extends your search to cover more ground.

Children may not be capable of telephoning places of contact with the appropriate questions and detail, but they should be encouraged to become involved in the search and kept updated.

Coping with the Loss

Know that your pet did not purposely run away from you. When pets run away, they are usually following their instinct to chase another animal or to wander the land and follow the scents of other living creatures. Pets do not run away from loving homes because they no longer love. The exchange of love and devotion between pet guardian and pet is far too great.

Your pet will always love you. There is no question of this. Understand and accept that something caught your pet's attention and triggered an instinct that caused his or her sudden disappearance.

Replacing a runaway or stolen pet for the sake of your children, or yourself, can be a positive action. But remember, your entire family needs time to grieve. It is essential that this be done before another pet is brought into the home. Grief and its attendant emotions should be allowed to surface for the health of body, mind and spirit.

If your runaway or stolen pet is not returned, know in your heart that you've done the best you could. Constant worrying about your pet's well-being will shadow you, but it is important to consider that your pet may have been found by another loving home. This does happen in many cases. After you have done your best to locate your pet, there is nothing more you can do but hope for your pet's safety and happiness.

Using Ritual to Cope with the Loss

In order to endure the emotional roller coaster of loss and begin the search for your loved one, you must maintain inner energy and strength. Gathering every ounce of strength within when the reality around you seems to be deteriorating is not an easy task. The feeling of loss is not only focused upon the physical absence of your pet, but includes the unpleasant sense that a loss of control has disrupted your life. Faith is challenged as we struggle to understand "why," in disbelief and utter dismay.

The cycles of life and nature are mysterious to us. We know that every ending is also a new beginning. This is true not only of physical death, but also of pet bereavement caused by runaway or stolen pets. The reasons for the disappearance may be mysterious, but your pet has not disappeared from the web of life. There is always hope for a reunion—upon the physical plane and beyond. Your communion with your pet is not merely a physical one. Your loving bond exceeds time and space. As with the loss of a pet through physical death, you need to accept that your relationship with your pet has gone through a cycle of transition.

You will journey within and outside of yourself for a sense of understanding. Now is a time when spiritual faith and strength are needed the most. You may feel that these are undermined by the questions you have asked of your deity that seem to have gone unanswered. You may wonder why the precious love of your pet has been taken away. It doesn't seem fair.

Ritual allows for soul searching and exploring the unknown in search of answers. Through ritual, we gain a clearer understanding of life, a rejuvenation of self. We begin building the foundation to regain control of our lives through spirituality and strengthening of self.

Self-exploratory rites to understand and touch the core of your inner resources can benefit you the most at this trying time. Healing rites can help you overcome your grief and continue healthy living. The ritual below combines both functions for a doubled effect of inner healing and reclaiming emotional strength.

This is also a ritual of psychic connection with your pet. Separation from your pet, whether in life or through physical death, causes feelings of love loss. It is natural to wish to rekindle the contact with your pet in some manner.

In our hearts we know that love forever binds us to those who are dear to us, whether or not they are with us. Your memories, your pet's memory and the power of love combine in an eternal nexus. Depending upon your personal and spiritual beliefs, it can be said that so long as you keep your memories and love, your pet is forever with you in spiritual union. The longing you have to experience that bond again can be gratified by psychic connecting.

Psychic and ritual work spiritually connects you with your pet. Communion through the medium of love and the life force in all creatures makes this possible.

I cannot assure you that conducting such a ritual will result in your pet's return home if he or she is missing. But, in experiencing the loving bond that will exist between you and your pet even through this separation, you will come to accept the loss and work toward resolution.

You may conduct this ritual ceremonially or casually. Casting a magic circle or following preparation procedures of your spiritual practice is ideal for connecting with your deity, empowering your faith and reclaiming inner strength.

Ritual of Pet Psychic Connection

The purpose of this ritual is to prompt self-healing and to make psychic contact with your lost or stolen pet. The ritual can project energies of protection to your lost pet and assist you in regaining a sense of control, revitalizing your faith and maintaining your connection with your pet.

What You'll Need

- Dried mugwort (*artemesia vulgaris*; you can purchase fresh leaves of this herb at health food stores, through herb mail-order catalogs or at New Age shops. Historically in folk magic this herb has been associated with the moon and the realm of the seer)

- A bowl
- A rattle or drum
- Your choice of incense
- Candles
- Your pet's personal belongings

Preparation

Schedule your ritual for a time when you can have privacy. The ritual can be conducted indoors or outdoors. Wear comfortable clothing. Avoid being interrupted by the phone or by other people who are not involved in the ritual.

Set up a temporary altar with the mugwort, incense to burn for purification, the rattle or drum, candles and your pet's personal belongings, which will aid you in acquiring psychic connection.

Open your sacred space with prayer or purification if desired. After doing so, take a seat in the center of your sacred space. Meditate for a moment on the purpose of your ritual and what you hope to gain from it. Concentrate upon your pet's safe return home and, simultaneously, on your own state of being, to generate strength, faith and the ability to emotionally cope.

Place the rattle or drum and mugwort leaves on the floor or ground in the center of your sacred space.

Hold the rattle or drum and stand in the center of your sacred space, facing north. (North is the sacred direction where the sun passes at night and represents the depths of the unconscious mind.

This direction is ideal for your psychic work.) Pivot sunwise once (turning east, south, west, and north again), shaking your rattle or beating your drum and visualizing the creation of an inner circle around your being. This serves to cleanse and purify yourself and your sacred space, and to construct a shield against negative or obstructing energy in preparation for your psychic work.

Return to facing north. Shake your rattle or beat your drum downward from your chest toward the floor to invoke the northern element of Earth and open the passage into Mother Earth. You may choose a prayer, or speak words such as:

"By the gift of earthly power given to me of Mother Earth, I open the passage of unseen natural power. By this, the first channel is opened."

Visualize white streams of energy entering the soles of your feet and flowing up your entire being. Feel their warmth, vibration and energy.

Stand in the center of your sacred space. Play your instrument at your chest to open the passage into your inner self and speak sacred words, such as:

"Empowered by my ancestors and the divine wisdom of God (or Goddess), I gather strength within me and break the ties that bind me consciously to this material world. By this, the second channel, the passage to my higher self, is opened."

Feel yourself open within. Your own energies are swirling in the streams of white light from Mother Earth. You may feel a lightness or a tickling sensation in your chest.

Raise your instrument to the heavens. Open the passage to the upper, spiritual world, and speak sacred words, such as:

"Through the divine power granted to me by God (or Goddess), I open the sacred passage to the spirit world. Hence, the sacred trinity of channels has been opened. I stand in the center of Universal Oneness and the Web of Life."

Visualize golden light streaming quickly from above you and entering into the crown of your head. Feel the warm, pulsating energy course through your entire being.

Sit down. White and gold swirls of combined earth energy and celestial energy circle you. Continue to rattle or drum in a rhythmic beat. Listen to the entrancing beat of your instrument. The rhythmic sound is symbolic of the divine heartbeat of all existence. Feel your own energy weaving into the earth and celestial energies. Clear your mind for a moment, and feel your mind unfold from the physical restraints of this world.

Stop playing your instrument and set it gently down beside you. Take the dried mugwort leaves into your hand. Sit comfortably in the center of your sacred space. Between your thumb and index finger, crush the leaves and say:

"By Mother Earth's gift of mugwort, the shadowy world of
the seer opens to me. Sacred herb of the ancient seers,
like my ancestors, I bathe in your essence. I cross oceans
of time—guide me through the sacred, psychic channels."

Crushing the mugwort between your thumb and index finger
relaxes your conscious mind and awakens your deep
consciousness. Rub the leaves together in front of your nose—not
directly beneath it. Gently inhale the aroma but do not inhale the
mugwort. (Inhaling the odor of the fresh, crushed leaves with
visualization promotes psychic awareness.[1] Please note, however,
that the essential oil of mugwort is hazardous and is not
recommended for use.)

Visualize the physical world around you melting away, and a
peaceful, celestial environment of unlimited darkness and stars
surrounding you—swallowing you. This is the realm of Universal
Oneness. Allow yourself to be totally absorbed. You feel that
everything is a part of you, and you are a part of everything in
existence.

Sprinkle the mugwort into the bowl on your altar. Calm your
conscious mind, releasing your daily worries and mundane
concerns. Relax your body and mind. Continue to visualize the
vast darkness of space and glittering stars, and the white and gold
streams of universal energy circling your being.

Sit with your spine straight and your head up to align your
cervical spine. Lower your shoulders. Allow your muscles to
relax. Rest your weary mind. Visualize and feel the heavens
surrounding you.

When your mind has unfolded and unconscious levels opened, you may feel a sense of projecting out of your physical body. This is to be expected.

Stop visualizing. Clear your mind completely. Only peace and clarity surround you. Rest for a moment. Next, visualize a mist that develops, then slowly dissipates. You find yourself in the midst of an extravagant garden. Visualize the sacred garden. You are seated upon moist, fertile, rich soil. Surrounding you is a labyrinth of green shrubbery and endless flowers of exquisite, unworldly beauty. The flowers around you are of unique composition and vibrant, individual colors. Before you is a separate bed of nine flowers, in three rows of three. You are within the Heavenly Garden, which offers healing and wisdom.

Each flower is a different species, with individual properties to assist you in the healing and psychic connection with your pet. Visualize them arranged in three rows:

First Row

Flower	Attribute
Red rose	Love, strength, vitality
Gold lily	Acceptance of transformation in life
Black iris	Absorption of fear

Second Row

Flower	Attribute
Purple pansy	Guidance toward resolution
Blue violet	Calm of emotions, perception
Green ivy	Intuition, inner healing

Third Row

Flower	Attribute
White mum	Peace, revitalization of higher self
Yellow gladiolus	Protection of a loved one
Orange marigold	Adaptability to transformation

Gazing upon the beauty of the flower bed, pick each flower whose qualities are needed for your balance and healing. The flowers project positive qualities for your absorption so that you may prepare for the psychic communion with your pet. You can only be of strength or guidance to your pet after first conjuring these qualities in yourself.

Visualize the streaming colors of the energy each flower emits being absorbed into your being. You breathe deeply the sweet, refreshing fragrance of the garden. The color rays are warm, protective and revitalizing to your soul.

Sit with your gathered flowers. Concentrate upon each and the qualities each provides you. Allow yourself to begin internal healing.

Know that you and your pet are eternally bound in spirit, in psychic mind, and in the divine realm of your deity. Know that although your physical life together has been abruptly ended, nothing can destroy the love you and your pet have forever.

Meditate on positive thoughts. Find acceptance within yourself. Note the transformation from the physical bond of love with your pet to a spiritual, psychic bond. There has been no end to life and love, but a new beginning in which you both will adapt and continue to love.

Lay your chosen flowers on the rich, dark soil next to you. Their amplified energies have made you feel strong and rejuvenated in mind and body. You are ready to make the psychic connection with your pet.

Visualize the fertile, brown soil of the garden before you caving inward beneath the blossoms. The flowers disappear in the shifting, sinking soil. An enormous hole is revealed in the earth. A tunnel of twisting roots, earthworms, and quartz crystals forms. The tunnel represents your separation, but also the undying love and connection you and your pet have against all odds.

Rise to your knees and lower yourself into the dark earth. Having projected from your physical shell, it is no struggle for you to travel the winding, rough soil tunnel. Once you reach the other end of the tunnel, you are united with your pet's aura. Now is the time to send messages, strength, positive energies and love to your pet. Take as much time as you need.

Allow your feelings to surface. Communicate to your pet the loss you feel, and your love. Do not make unrealistic promises that you may not be able to keep. Promising success may lead to guilt and regret later if you are unable to find your pet. State that you'll do everything in your power to locate and reunite with your pet; this is a legitimate promise.

When you have completed your communication with your pet, send a final message that the communication is near its end. You can always renew yourself at heaven's garden, or visit your pet through the tunnel again in the future.

In closing the ritual, you may simply end with a moment of meditation and reflection. You may wish to write your experience in a journal.

Many people who have practiced this ritual claim to reunite with their pet in a "light body." Some individuals have visualized themselves and their pet as separate auras of flowing energy. Others state that ghostly spirit doubles of their physical bodies reunited at the tunnel's end. How you envision your reunion with your pet is a unique, intimate experience. You may sense your pet's presence, or visualize him or her.

Do not be concerned that psychic communication, or the reunion through the tunnel, may confuse or upset your pet should he or she be in another person's care, or adjusting to a new environment. In my opinion, any positive, unselfish energies and psychic transmittal you provide can only benefit your pet. You may receive messages from your pet that will ease your mind in knowing he or she is happy and well.

Ritual will help you to heal and strengthen yourself, enabling you to celebrate forever the loving bond between you and your pet.

Ritual is meant to be a positive action toward understanding, acceptance and healing. If you continue to dwell upon negative thoughts about your pet's disappearance, which may or may not reflect reality, you will prolong your grief and miss the opportunity to continue to enjoy the love you share. Rejoice in the memories, hope for the best and celebrate your eternal love.

9

Rituals and Meditations

IN THIS CHAPTER, YOU'LL FIND SEVERAL RITUALS AND MEDITATIONS that can help release negative feelings as well as prompt healing, emotional stability, balance and spiritual flow of positive energies. The Cleansing the Gate ritual symbolically marks the beginning of a new, spiritual state of existence for your beloved pet. The Crossing the Bridge ritual I created for individuals of different spiritual beliefs who have solicited my counsel during this time of transformation in their relationship with their beloved pet.

Deciding on a Ceremony

In thinking about whether or not to have a wake, funeral or religious death ceremony for your pet, consider what you desire and what you wish to avoid. If your family does not feel a ceremony is appropriate, plan a later ceremony for yourself at the burial site, or with friends of like mind.

If your pet is cremated, you can bury his or her ashes or scatter them in a sacred space. Some individuals choose to keep their beloved pet's ashes inside their home in a decorative urn or container. If your pet is cremated, keeping the ashes allows you to conduct a ceremony at your convenience and with the additional flexibility and privacy that home burial can offer.

These rites, or rites that you create, will not rid you of the emotional distress that must accompany your grief. The rites are meant to help you recognize, accept and feel better about the transformation of your life that occurs with the loss of your pet's physical presence, and to assist your pet through his or her transition into the spirit world. Most actions in the rituals are symbolic of nature, and each one acts as its own spell to see that your wishes for your pet are carried out.

Death ceremonies symbolize an end to one stage of your life and the beginning of another. Everything around you seems to have changed—and much of it has. This is the time to be joyous that your pet's soul journeys to heavenly freedom from the struggles of physical existence.

The Beginning

In every ending, there is a beginning. Our lives wax and wane like the changing seasons and the turning cosmos. Death holds within it a bright hope for eternal life in spirit and reunion. Although the period of coping is difficult, it is also a time of change, transformation and rebirth of self.

In Chapter 2 we discussed the nature of death, including theories of reincarnation and forms of rebirth. These theories are important in this chapter, because they are the backbone of the rituals and meditations. No matter what your spiritual practice, you can apply your own theories and beliefs regarding death and the afterlife during these exercises.

In Chapter Three, you were encouraged to put your pet's belongings into storage for a short time immediately following his or her death. In this chapter, we'll use a ceremony to ritually cleanse your home and the space shared with your pet. This ceremony exerts positive energies, purifies your surroundings and eases the unexpected transformation. It also begins a natural cycle that frees your pet's spirit toward divinity, peace and freedom, and allows him or her to pass between the physical world and the spiritual world at any time.

How can such a ritualistic cleansing be helpful? In temporarily cleansing your home of the physical objects and reminders that upset you, you begin the healing cycle of acceptance of change. As you accept the transformation, you will begin to heal and realize that your pet's soul is free. By cleansing your home, you usher your pet's soul into heaven. His or her soul is free to find sanctuary in heaven, spiritual freedom and eventual rebirth.

In performing this ritual, you are not casting out your pet's presence from your life. At this moment, you need to recognize and accept the transformation of your pet's being. By performing these rituals, you mark your understanding and accept that this transformation has already begun and must now be completed. These are healthy exercises that allow you to move through the stages of grief without constant reminders of the physical being and presence your pet once shared with you. It is time to begin a spiritual and esoteric relationship with your pet.

Cleansing the Gate

Throughout history humans have told mythological stories of a gate between our physical existence and the spiritual world. In Greek mythology, this gate exists in Hades, "the Unseen," the netherworld in which the Lord of Death, whom the Greeks revered in order to secure the spiritual condition of departed souls, rules.[1] The Greeks believed that after a proper burial, the deceased arrive at one of the rivers of Hades, Styx or Acheron, where Charon, the ferryman of the dead, rows them across. Cerberus, the hound, guards the gate of Hades and protects its souls.

Ancient Egyptian religion symbolizes the gate between the physical and spiritual worlds as a ladder that a person must erect on the God Geb (the earth) and climb until reaching the Goddess Nut (the sky). This ladder was said to help the deceased ascend to heaven.[2]

The gate symbolizes our efforts to visualize a physical connection between our world and the spiritual realm. The concept provides a sense of recognition and understanding that we each must pass through the gate in time. It is our life destiny.

The purpose of the Cleansing the Gate ritual is to purify your emotional state and your physical realm. As it purifies, the ritual helps you to accept the death, allowing the transformation and beginning the healing process. Many individuals consider this ritualistic activity a way to help a beloved pet into the awaiting divinity of the Supreme Being. The ritual can be a reassurance that your passing pet's soul will indeed be graced with ease in the spiritual journey toward its heavenly destination.

What You'll Need

- Storage boxes to temporarily hold your pet's belongings
- Two vessels or glasses, one filled with salt and the other with water or holy water

Optional

- Soothing music
- Incense
- Candles
- Matches

Preparations

If you live with another individual or with your family, you may ask them to join you in this exercise. If you feel this ritual is too intimate to share, conduct it alone.

Unplug the telephone, draw the shades, and turn off the television and radio. Surround yourself with reassuring privacy and peace. Peace is the necessary ingredient to this exercise.

Feel free to conduct this ritual as ceremonially or casually as you prefer. Alter it to meet your spiritual needs.

Vacuum, dust, wash windows and tidy your living space—especially the areas most frequently traveled by your deceased pet. Move furniture around and redecorate as you wish. The change that has occurred in your life needs to be recognized, accepted and adapted to. Physically moving furniture greatly helps this transformation.

Leave your pet's belongings where they rest for this moment in the ritual. You may arrange a temporary altar that consists of ritual tools you use during your spiritual practice.

Set the vessels of salt and water on the table or altar within the room your pet was in most often. Take a few moments to stand or sit and meditate.

Ask your deity for compassion and guidance as you cope with the loss of your beloved animal companion. Express aloud to your deity exactly what you desire for your pet, such as, "It is my deepest desire that Sheba be embraced within the nurturing arms of the Heavenly Father and that He graciously accept my little one into His divine realm to exist happily, painlessly, and as divine until I am reunited with her," or, "I wish for Duke to unite with God and become as one with the cosmic powers of the universe until such time as he may be granted the renewal of rebirth."

No matter how lengthy your request, use this time to express those feelings within your heart. If you become upset, allow yourself to cry and release your sorrow. At this very moment you are telling your deity that you've recognized your pet's death as reality and you now wish to accept it and speak your expectations for your pet's spiritual transformation. There will be tears and emotional pain, but you are moving from the earliest stages of grief toward healing.

When you've spoken your true feelings and wishes, tell yourself, "It shall be," or something similar, such as, "It is done." This marks the end of your worrying and dwelling upon your pet's soul as it journeys. You've told your deity your wishes, and now you know they will be granted. This is the moment when you invoke your love and trust in your deities to help you cope. The time has come to proceed with your life and in some ways to begin anew.

Take a pinch of salt with your thumb and forefinger. Rub your fingers together over the water vessel, sprinkling the salt generously into the water. If other people are included in this ritual, have them recite a special poem or speak as they wish as you mix the salt and water.

Sprinkle the mixture throughout the room. As you do this, you or a partner can recite a prayer, or repeat a phrase such as, "With salt and water I do cleanse; through (your pet's name)'s death his/her new life begins." By repeating these words you are ritualistically marking an end to the physical life you shared with your pet. You have now accepted that your pet must begin a new life—not necessarily separated from you, but new and different nonetheless.

When you finish sprinkling the purifying and cleansing mixture in one room, proceed to the next room. Dash the mixture upon your pet's belongings. This cleansing of your pet's possessions symbolizes your approval of your pet's new spiritual existence.

Do not rush the cleansing. If you become emotionally upset, continue. This is the time to express your feelings. Release your emotions freely. Many times, people feel that by expressing sorrow they are hurting others or causing others to feel bad. If you are reciting a prayer and are unable to continue because of your tears, then allow yourself to stop the recital and simply continue the cleansing. If you or other individuals present show sadness and despair, then this ritual has served a purpose. If any of those present become upset, embrace them. Hug your child lovingly, and take hold of your spouse's hand, or embrace your partner. Human beings need to feel and experience the warmth, understanding and love we can give one another at times of bereavement. We need to share and experience these emotions together.

Once each room your pet occupied has been cleansed, including his or her belongings, place the salt and water vessels on a table to await disposal.

If others are present, join hands to form a circle. Allow each person to speak a farewell or wishes for the departed pet. This is a wonderful exercise for the entire family. Each member can speak his or her feelings aloud and the experience is shared intimately. Encourage young children to say whatever they feel. Keep a compassionate and attentive environment as each person speaks.

If you are alone, take this moment to speak again if you feel the need. Think of your fond memories, consider how your pet would wish you to live without him or her and make a promise to your pet and yourself to move forward.

Afterward, place your pet's belongings in the storage boxes. Remind yourself that this is temporary—you can bring out the belongings when you have learned to live with the now spiritual and esoteric relationship you share with your pet. When you enter the final stages of grief, you can use a shelf or table in one of the rooms to create a memorial, complete with all your pet's belongings, photographs and more.

Burial and Cremation Funeral Ceremonies

Whether your pet is to be buried at home or at a pet cemetery, or cremated at a facility, you can conduct a funeral ceremony. Many psychologists, animal lovers and pet bereavement counselors see such ceremonies as highly beneficial and healthy. It is normal to express your sorrow and love by saying farewell to the animal friend whose life filled yours with unconditional love and devotion.

If you plan arrangements at a pet cemetery or crematorium, ask employees if you can view your pet beforehand and hold a wake or funeral ceremony. Unless the staff is callous or insensitive, they should agree to your request. If you are refused, leave and take your pet elsewhere. There is no reason you shouldn't have privacy with your family, friends and pet before any proceedings. Some facilities and cemeteries, however, may charge an additional fee for this request.

Facilities for burial and cremation usually have "viewing rooms" or private areas you can use to spend time with your pet before burial or cremation. In the case of burial, you will also have the opportunity to be present for the entire process—even to the point of having your pet's grave marker installed after burial. In cremation, after the initial private moments, you usually will not have another opportunity to conduct a ceremony until the cremation is complete.

Crossing the Bridge

Crossing the Bridge is a death and rebirth ritual used to prompt the deceased to cross the bridge between the physical and spiritual worlds. After finding sanctuary in the spiritual world, he or she will be able to return to the physical world as desired. "Crossing the Bridge" is the term associated with all traditions of contemporary nature-revering religions, such as Wicca, and is meant to be performed for the deceased human loved one. It can be slightly altered, however, to provide ritualistic guidance for your deceased pet.

You can conduct this rite indoors or outdoors. It is ideal for home burial, burial at a pet cemetery or cremation. Format your own ritual if you wish, and write your own wording.

What You'll Need
- Candles
- Incense and fireproof container
- Flowers
- A bell
- An altar (physical or visualized)

Preparation
Dress in comfortable clothes, or, if you like, in a ceremonial robe with religious jewelry. You can carry your robe and jewelry in a bag to the facility.

Usually there is at least one table in the viewing room where you may set up your temporary altar. Candles can be carefully placed on the floor or around the room. Flowers are always beautiful and symbolic of the beauty of life and rebirth.

If you have chosen burial at a pet cemetery, your pet may be in his or her casket, behind closed doors. Usually, an employee opens the casket before you enter. Before beginning the ritual, be certain that your pet is in the casket; sometimes the grooming that your pet receives before being placed in the casket takes longer than expected.

Ask someone from your group to ring the bell at the beginning of the ritual. The speaking parts below include the woman (yourself or your wife, mother, daughter etc.), the man (yourself or your husband, father, son etc.) and All (yourself, your spouse, friends, and anyone else in attendance). Make necessary adjustments to suit your needs.

The ritual begins with all present standing within a circle, surrounded by candles and flowers. The appointed person must ring the bell to begin.

Individual who sounds the bell: "The bell has been sounded in the honor of our beloved (your pet's name)."

All: "In expressing our love."

Woman: "Today we, the loved ones of (pet's name) have gathered. (Pet's name) is no longer physically with us, and we all are deeply saddened. We deeply miss our beloved. We call upon our Lord to help us cope. We must not be sad, for we know birth is destined for death, and the beauty of all life must inevitably wane for a time through transformation of the departed soul. Shall we not smile through tears of joy rather than tears of sadness? Has our beloved's death not been a sign from our divine deity that his/her life's work has been fulfilled? Now through death he/she evolves. No longer are pain, suffering and the struggles of life upon him/her. We shall all be reunited eternally, do not fear. That reunion is much awaited and greatly coveted, and will be a glorious time of celebration."

Man: "Present in (pet's name)'s honor, we send forth blessings and wishes as we help him/her across the Bridge to heaven. The Bridge is eternally present for him/her to return, at any time, as desired to be with us here who so cherish his/her love."

All present should raise their open palms toward heaven, in the direction of the altar, to send energies symbolically across the Bridge.

At this time, each person imagines the deceased, beloved pet appearing as best remembered while alive—healthy, happy and joyous. The participants can touch hands, if desired. This concentrates energies of love, joy and happiness that will be projected from their bodies and sent through the fingertips into the beloved pet's body. The sending of energies continues for a few moments.

Woman: "The unconditional love, devotion and happiness you've touched our lives with will never be forgotten. As you know, we will never forget the love, devotion and happiness we shared with you. When we wish to meet you upon the Bridge, we will do so in our sacred space (church, temple, circle etc.), in dreams and within our hearts. You are forever welcome. We wish you love, happiness and freedom from the restraints of physical existence."

All: *(holding hands)* "Love is eternal. Love is divine. Forever we shall be bonded in spirit."

The rite has ended. Individuals may choose to approach your pet to bid farewell and have intimate communion. The remaining time should be spent remembering the deceased pet by speaking of happy and joyous times and memorable moments. Finally, the ritual activity is brought to a close. Extinguish the candles and put away any decorations. Your pet's transformation, and the transformation in your life, is complete.

Meditations

The following meditation exercises can help you emotionally, psychologically and spiritually each day. They are simple and do not require yoga experience or expertise. Each one takes about an hour. It is essential that you make the necessary time to meditate—no excuses. Notify housemates that you need to have one hour of uninterrupted privacy.

Before beginning either of these meditations, you need to focus and quiet your conscious mind with a premeditation ritual. This ritual will also prepare your entire subconscious to awaken with action.

Pre-Meditation Ritual

What You'll Need

- Incense (sandalwood, myrrh or frankincense is ideal, but any incense of a flowery, fruity or light, pleasing aroma is perfect)

- Candles
- Matches
- A drum

Preparations

For your quiet hour of meditation, choose a room in your home or an area outdoors. Use a table as your altar. Set up the candles. Light the incense. If indoors, eliminate all other light sources when lighting the candles.

Seated before the candles, inhale deeply, pause momentarily and exhale slowly. Inhale again deeply, hold for a count of four, and exhale slowly. For a few moments, just continue to relax. Allow the aroma of the incense to shift your consciousness, and the silence to bring peace into your mourning. Relax. Clear your conscious mind of worries.

If you have a drum, this would be a perfect time to use it. At this stage of the meditation you are preparing to gradually still the mind, shift your consciousness and reach your inner self. A soft drumbeat, like a slow heartbeat, would be ideal during this phase. Close your eyelids, breathe in relaxation and listen to the heartbeat of your drum.

Acceptance Meditation

The purpose of this meditation is to help you in the recognition and acceptance of your pet's death and the transformation of your loving relationship. This meditation, unlike the meditation in Chapter Five, is for the purpose of healing yourself and does not include communication with your pet. If you are uncomfortable with this, you may alter the meditation to suit your personal needs and desires.

Whether drumming or not, imagine the rhythm of a heartbeat. Listen and release yourself from worry and emotional turmoil.

Many individuals fail when attempting meditation because they do not know the correct technique. To attempt to overcome this problem we will continue with the relaxation breathing exercise and focus on our third eye. By focusing upon it you transcend association with your physical self and mental/conscious realizations. Concentrating upon the third eye, in the center of the forehead, allows you to arise beyond the conscious and subconscious cares of the physical and become aware of truth, or the true, divine source.

In shamanic healing the third eye is related to the sacred Six, the power of the ancestors. Through the concentration of the third eye, we can understand the spiritual connection, the web of life, between all sentient beings and souls. We invoke the assistance of ancestors who have waited to help us after having fulfilled their own earthly lives. Ancestors and departed loved ones await your summons. When you focus upon the third eye, help will be granted for you to cross the threshold into the spirit world, enabling you to spiritually connect with your pet.

Seated, keep your head straight and comfortably aligned, with shoulders relaxed and back. Do not let your head tilt forward. Keep your neck straight. Look upward, but do not tilt your head back to look up at the ceiling or sky; rather keep your head straight and look upward only with your eyes (the lids may be open or closed). How do you feel after a moment of rhythmic breathing and focusing on your third eye? You should feel a sense of spiritual enlightenment and expansion. You are soaring above the horizon and concentrating upon your higher, spiritual consciousness. You are free from the physical realm.

You can sit or lie down for this next exercise. Choose a position in which your spine does not curve, your muscles do not tighten and you are comfortable. If you are lying down, placing a pillow beneath your lower thighs or knees will help keep your spine straight.

Breathe. If you have been drumming softly, cease. Allow your arms and hands to lie softly on your lap. Sit upright and stretch your body. Reach for the sky with your arms, and stretch your legs outward like tree roots in search of water. Now, taking your time, do some physical relaxation exercises.

Carefully let your head fall forward so that your chin touches your chest. Breathe in, count four, then slowly exhale. Lift your head upright.

Leaning your head to the left, gently tip it as far as possible. Take your right arm and place it behind you with your forearm against your lower back. Hold momentarily. Feel your arm's position helping to lightly stretch and relax your neck and shoulder muscles. Inhale, count four and exhale. Resume your upright position.

Tip your head as far as possible to the right. Place your left arm behind your back with your forearm against your lower back. Carefully stretch. Inhale, count four, exhale. Resume the upright position of your head.

Breathe normally. Allow your head to slowly fall forward, right, back, and left. Do so gently, without strain. Repeat, but this time have your head fall to your chest, tip left, fall back, tip right, and come upright.

Upon completion of these exercises you should feel wonderfully refreshed, with a renewed sense of calm and balance. If not, you should slowly perform the exercises again until your body and mind at least feel free from tension.

Next, bend your arms slightly and lift them so that your hands are held approximately fifteen to eighteen inches away from your chest. Stretch out your fingers so that your palms face away from your body. Your fingers and hands should not be rigid or tense. Simply face your palms away from you.

Breathe normally and absorb the warmth of the candle flames into your palms. Close your eyes if you wish. The warmth is symbolic of your deity's love and understanding of your sorrow at the death of your beloved pet. Soon the warmth will be absorbed through your hands, down your arms and into your body, providing nurturing heat that loosens your tensed muscles and mind.

The candle's flame, or a hearth fire, has been used as a focal point in meditation and divination for ages. With concentration of your consciousness, this practice can induce a mediumistic trance. Sit before the candle flames now and allow the element of fire to weave its spell as you meditate upon your beloved pet. Do not take this moment to further emotionally distress yourself in desiring your pet's return. You need to accept the transformed relationship and bond that you share.

When you are ready, come out of the meditation slowly. Return gently, allowing your conscious mind to awaken. Offer thanks to your deity for the spiritually cleansing experience. The spirit of your pet dwells upon planes that are relatively close to our physical plane of existence. Know in your heart that you will always be connected to your pet in spirit, and that this new relationship offers the opportunity to celebrate your undying love.

Seven Wheels toward Healing Meditation
This is a healing meditation that uses the chakras.

Chakras represent a complex system for spiritual development beyond what is covered herein. I recommend you read more extensive material to fully appreciate and understand their purpose. There is a wealth of information available about the chakras and their uses, and in the Suggested Reading section of this book I recommend several excellent sources for your study.

Eastern religions have always worked with energy centers of the body, and the chakra system greatly helps practitioners develop control over these centers. To assist you in your healing work, you will be using the seven classical chakra centers most popularly taught in yoga.

In the Eastern texts the chakras are illustrated in beautiful images of lotus flowers. Flowers are an evocative analogy for the chakras, as they can be closed, in bud, open or blossoming depending on whether they are active or dormant.[3] In Sanskrit, the word chakra means "wheel," and chakras spin like individual wheels in relation to the degree of energy in the system of the individual.[4]

Physical illness, emotional distress and daily stress can disrupt the chakras and cause physical and/or psychosomatic symptoms. Our aim is to cleanse, stimulate and balance the chakras toward healing your distress. Our exercise will restore balance to the chakras and develop their energies, which will benefit you physically, emotionally and intellectually as you strive to cope with your pet's death.

What You'll Need
- Comfortable clothing
- Pillow
- Incense
- Scented lotion or essential oil. Native American medicine herbs, such as sage, are ideal. Apply the scented lotion or essential oil at pressure points (wrists, neck, ankles and the back of your head). You will want to combine the benefits of aromatherapy and natural, herbal incense in this session.

Preparation
No music should be played. Instruments for visual stimulation (candles, statues, etc.) are not necessary unless you so desire.

Seat yourself upon the pillow, on the floor. Your legs can be resting in "Indian style" or however they are most comfortable, so they will not ache or numb. If sitting is not ideal, then arrange several pillows to allow for lying on the floor. A bed or couch is not ideal, because you do not want to go to sleep. You are striving to isolate yourself from secular activity, to reach deep within to the center of your energy for stimulation toward healing. Sitting or lying down in an unusual place, like the floor, will help your mind become more aware.

Once seated, begin by focusing on your breathing. Allow your chest and abdomen to expand fully as you inhale deeply. There is no need to tighten your muscles when you exhale; allow your muscles to contract naturally. To develop rhythmic breathing for relaxation, calming of the body and focusing of the mind, inhale and hold your breath for a count of four, then slowly exhale over four beats. Fill your lungs. Take pleasure in the inhalation of the sweet oxygen of life, then release the carbon dioxide slowly. This concentrated breathing is often termed "centering." You should practice first, then continue centering throughout this session.

Within your mind identify your "three selves": your conscious mind, which feels your emotional responses to your pet's death; your inner child, who likes to playfully recall the good times spent with your pet; and lastly your "higher self," who feels your spiritual beliefs and intentions. Identify the trinity and connect the three. Bring them to full awareness in your mind and momentarily give attention to each—appreciating them separately and loving yourself in all aspects as your pet unconditionally does.

Visualize an egg-shaped oval of light that surrounds your entire being. Examine this oval of light carefully to search for tears, cracks or negative abnormalities. Focus on each thought that presents itself. Thank each, and let it go. Release concerns, thoughts and ideas of the conscious mind that interrupt the process of attaining a meditative state of mind.

Once done, take a moment to check that your spine is straight, whether you are sitting or lying down. This will be most important as we begin working with the chakras. Now visualize one trapdoor at the bottom of the oval aura and another at the top. Open each trapdoor visually and notice that each has a mesh-like screening so that no "lower" or negative vibrations can enter—only "higher" or positive vibrations are pure enough to penetrate the fine mesh. This screening can also be used to filter psychic debris and rid your aura of their presence. Visualize particles of dirt or debris, representing negativity, trauma and emotional distress, being freed from your being. Mentally push these unwanted particles upwards and out through the top trapdoor. Continue until all the debris is gone and you feel cleansed.

From the bottom trapdoor, sense the gravity that holds your being upon the earth. Feel the earth's energies alive and healing. Draw these energies from the Earth Mother in the form of warm, golden light that floods the oval-shaped bubble of your aura just as water is poured into a glass. An alternative combination of colors, lavender followed by silver (a healing combination thought to clean accumulated "etheric debris" from the chakras), can also be used instead of golden light. Use your intuition. Continue drawing on these energies, imagining them streaming upward from the roots and caverns of the molten core of the earth. The stream of energies brings renewal, clarity of mind and the healing benefits of positive, natural energies. Once the earth's healing forces have energized your body, push them downward—sending them back to the molten core of the earth. This procedure is typically termed "grounding" and cleanses, balances and stimulates the energies within your aura.

After a few moments, draw a pearlesque white light energy from the top trapdoor. This is the plasma of the universe. Allow it to flood your aura and surround your being as you did with the golden light of the Earth Mother energies. Once it fills your aura completely, release it through the bottom trapdoor, in a rose or green light, down into the depths of the Earth Mother. (Do not use another color of universal energy from the top trapdoor. Doing so might short-circuit your chakra system and cause unwanted eruptions of energies within individual or all chakras. All color is a physical manifestation of energy, and the vibratory rate of light is determined and differentiated by the color ray; hence the color signifies the type of energy being accessed.) Once this phase is complete, you will cleanse the chakras individually.

Chakra Color and Bodily Location

Below is a chart illustrating the location of chakras within the body and the color used to represent them in all applications of magical, meditational and healing procedures. Use this chart to navigate as we continue.

Drawing the universal energies in through the top trapdoor and releasing them through the bottom trapdoor to the earth causes each chakra to begin turning, like small spoked wheels. Using the chart above, identify each chakra and visualize yourself using a soft, plush cloth to gingerly wipe each chakra. Wipe in a clockwise motion, as this is the direction a chakra should spin.

CHAKRA CHART

Chakra	Color	Location
First	Red	The base of your spine, coccyx, between your legs
Second	Orange	Below your navel, in line with your sacrum
Third	Yellow	Your solar plexus; stomach area
Fourth	Green	The middle of your chest; the thymus/heart
Fifth	Blue	Your throat/thyroid
Sixth	Indigo/Violet	Your pineal gland; between your brows and above your eyes
Seventh	Violet/White	At your crown; the top of your head/pituitary gland

Continue, until each chakra has been sufficiently cleansed and stimulated and is spinning strong and vibrant with the brilliance of its natural color. All debris and negative particles removed in this cleansing should be pushed upward through the top trapdoor, where they will be converted and neutralized into new universal energy.

At this time, call upon your deity to lend power to assist you. Choose a specific aspect of your deity that suits your purpose of

working toward healing. Any deity, angel or healer with whom
you work intimately in your spiritual practice is ideal. For
example, if you are Catholic, you may wish to choose Saint
Francis of Assisi for his remarkable work with animals. Every
religious mythology and ideology has one or more deities that can
offer exceptional benefits to a healing session focused upon death
and grief.

Once you've chosen your deity, continue to visualize yourself
within your egg-shaped aura, with chakras cleansed and spinning
vibrantly. The Earth Mother energy that you have drawn in is
contained within your root, the first chakra; and the universal
energies you have absorbed come down from your crown, the
seventh chakra, and invoke your personal energy through the
solar plexus, the third chakra. Blend the three types of energy
together. Visualize the combined energy as a mixture of pearl-
white light (universal energies), golden light (Earth Mother
energy), and streaming yellow light (your personal energy)
coming forth from the solar plexus, the third chakra.

Slightly bend and raise your arms and lift your hands upward,
palms facing away from your body. Take the combined three
energies into your palms. The energy vortices spinning on each of
your palms can be termed "lesser chakras." It is through these
lesser chakras that your magical healing energy is pushed out into
the physical plane and can be drawn upon to help your emotional
distress, ease the mourning process and otherwise support your
physical existence.

Concentrate and feel the combined power leaving your palms
and slowly filling the interior of your aura. You have successfully

cleansed the most important energy centers in your body, the chakras, and with the incorporation of both universal energies and Earth Mother energy you have charged them to healthy renewal, providing balance to your physical body and clarity of your mind.

With one final, strong release directed into your aura, create and visualize an explosion of energy that will direct the power to the astral and physical plane for your benefit. Push all of your energy down through your arms to exit your palms, combining your will, desire, emotion, concentration, visualization and every ounce of both physical and spiritual energy. Just as in magical workings, think of the beneficial energies that are working to heal you *now*—in the present tense. Will it, desire it, and bring the healing effects into being.

Keep your palm chakras open and receive the output of energies back through your palms, into your body. Feel them being re-absorbed into your solar plexus, third chakra. Visualize the streaming, glowing energies entering your palms, and feel the warmth and strength they deliver once contained within your solar plexus. "As above, so below"—both your subjective universe and your objective universe are receiving a blast of powerful, healing energy that will give you the extra strength you need to cope and internally heal.

To complete the meditation, re-position yourself so that you are on your knees, bending down until your forehead touches the ground (or floor), and place both palms on the ground on either side of your head. Rest in this position briefly to ground any excess energy back into the earth, then resume your previous position. The grounding is done.

Rest your arms upon your lap. Breathe deeply, using the breathing exercises recommended at the beginning of this meditation session. As you inhale, feel the renewal of positive energy fill your nostrils and lungs. Many individuals claim the air feels particularly chilly when the first inhale is done, while others claim it smells wonderfully pure and fresh. These are signs that the energies now existing in your aura and within you have combined properly. Rest momentarily. Energy play is tiring work, and you should pause to feel the energies surrounding you. Feel good, and know that these energies will help you cope and heal through this difficult time.

Thank your deity and the universal and Mother Earth energies.

Visualize the egg-shaped oval light surrounding your body becoming less and less visible as it descends back into your body. Gradually, your aura returns to its normal place within your being, where it remains until brought forth again for another healing, or for magical and ritual working. Separate the trinity of selves: your conscious mind, your inner child, and your higher self. Identify each separately, feeling its rejuvenation and renewed energy levels, then absorb these aspects into your mind. Stretch your body and resume normal breathing. Sit and allow your chemistry, muscles and energy to adjust. Your conscious mind will resume its usual activities, and its demands for attention. After a moment of reflection, close the session.

10

Pet Bereavement and Spirituality

THROUGHOUT THIS BOOK, WE'VE MENTIONED SPIRITUALITY. THIS chapter investigates how different spiritual belief systems view pet death.

You cannot discuss the subject of death without referring to spiritual beliefs. In most religions, we hope to unite with our deity or become divine in order to be granted an afterlife. All the religions of the world have sacred teachings regarding death; death is a magnet that pulls us closer to the divine through our spiritual practice.

Throughout history, our ancestors have sought understanding of and preparation for death through religion. Ages ago, the wise man/woman, medicine man/woman, clergy and appointed priesthoods of all civilizations were the only acknowledged authorities on the subject.

Today our lifestyles, attitudes and ideas about death have changed. Many individuals have beliefs about death and the afterlife that are not derived from a particular religious tradition. Science has given us new theories of human existence that affect our viewpoint of death as well as life. No longer is "hellfire and brimstone" considered the destiny of humanity. The fear of death has been used as a weapon or a manipulative tool to dominate those unwilling to conform to certain religious standards. These scare tactics have been discarded for the most part as individuals strive for their own sense of spirituality and divinity.

How do the world's religions understand and counsel pet loss? Pet loss is a relatively recent concern within many religions. Long ago, only the nobility and landed gentry kept pets for pleasure and companionship.[1] Gradually, as more people attained leisure and wealth, the keeping of pets for human pleasure became popular.

With the evolving interest in pet guardianship, public awareness about animal rights and various pet issues came into being. This created initial understanding of the human-pet bond. With the growing awareness of that loving bond arose the questions of many grieving pet lovers: What happens to my pet at death? Do animals have souls, and will they find sanctuary in the realm of the Gods? Will I be reunited with my pet in the afterlife? Historically, these questions were scoffed at and ignored.

Modern-day religious practitioners who have animal companions have introduced the question of what organized religion can do to help the deeply bereaved pet guardian. In some cases, a pet guardian asks a member of the clergy for compassion and counsel, and is told that help is not available. The different viewpoints described here provide a more universal and cross-cultural look into the ideology modern organized religion holds concerning the subject of pet death, grief for a pet and the human-pet bond.

Buddhism

The goal of the practitioner of Mahayana Buddhism is to lead all sentient beings to Supreme Freedom, an irreversible state of bliss that frees us from all suffering and its causes. In accepting this goal, the individual begins upon the path of spiritual development.

Mahayana Buddhism believes that all sentient beings have had countless rebirths. It is through this teaching that the practitioner considers all sentient beings, including animals, as having been mothers who have shown us great kindness. In our present life, we may not recognize them as our previous mothers, since we and they have been reborn into new life forms, but they have been our mothers many, many times and will continue to be.

Tibetan Buddhists believe that all sentient beings deserve kindness and the best care to keep them happy and healthy. There is a tradition in Tibet wherein individuals purchase animals that are about to be butchered and keep them instead as domestic pets. Saving the life of one such animal is considered to bring great healing to a sick person.

Holy shrines and temples in Tibet frequently are crowded with individuals walking their animals, since it is thought that an animal who sees a religious image, or hears the sound of prayers or teachings, will obtain the most favorable rebirth.

Buddhists read aloud daily prayers for their domestic pets and other animals to hear. It is thought to be especially helpful to recite the names of the Bodhisattvas and Buddhas to a dying animal. When an animal has died, holy people are requested to come and pray for the deceased. The bereaved owner can also go into the temple to pray for the animal and make offerings.

All sentient beings, whether human or animal, are believed to eventually attain the state of Supreme Freedom, Buddhahood. This is possible because the consciousness is ultimately separable from the defilements that in this life prevent the attainment of that state.

Buddhists understand the grief a pet guardian feels when a pet dies, but do not recommend dwelling upon sadness. They often suggest conducting religious practices, saying prayers and casting wishes to benefit the animal's cycle of rebirths and spiritual development.

Catholicism

The Catholic saint Francis of Assisi is one of the most important spiritual figures that can provide some consolation in pet loss. He loved all of God's creation, and devoted himself to God. He felt that we as human beings were meant to live in harmony with God, other living creatures and the whole of nature. After all, Christ was born in a manger surrounded by animals.

It may be worthwhile for you to study St. Francis during your grief; he was a man who lived and felt as you do. (See also Christianity, below.)

Christianity

The Christian Bible, or New Testament, does not contain any references to pets.[2] References are made to animals in general, to the utilitarian functions animals have served in our survival and to our responsibility to treat them humanely. We know through writings from ages ago that farm animals, and other animals who performed utilitarian functions, often shared shelter with their human owners. The concept of companion animals did not exist at the time when the Bible was written; the human-pet bond was a thing of the future.

Due to these facts, grieving pet guardians are often distressed to find that the Christian scriptures do not address pet loss. On its own, the Bible does not provide us with guidance on this issue. But there are Christian spiritual leaders who feel a genuine concern about the subject.

In general, the pet bereavement books I have read that were written by Christian authors refer to other belief systems, such as Native American or Eastern religions, in order to provide insight. In these traditions, you will recall, the death of a pet is respected as much as the death of a human.

Many Christian authors of pet bereavement books recommend that readers seek out the writings of the transcendental poets for their beautiful compassion and hope. Readers are also referred to the metaphysical philosophers, who emphasize teachings similar to those of the Eastern religions, such as reverence for nature.

When studying Christianity, we are reminded through Jesus Christ's death of the teaching of resurrection, and that new life is born of death. In modern Christianity, resurrection is seen as a new life born into heaven, or union with God. In your religious practice, you might consider that your pet's soul will be resurrected in heaven and will eventually be reunited with yours.

Christian theology is based upon a God of love that has created all life lovingly. The book of Genesis says that human beings are to be caretakers to the other creatures of God. Like God, we are to treat all life with the utmost love. Our responsibilities as human beings include sustaining loving relationships with all creatures.

The biblical story of Noah and the Ark describes God's covenant as made with all living creatures—not merely human beings. In many denominations of Christianity, leaders are trying to establish a better understanding of God's consideration for the human-pet bond by studying biblical references to animals and using them to counsel the bereaved.

There are many references within the scriptures to God grieving for the physical death of his creatures. Therefore, it is natural for you as a Christian to mourn your pet.

My suggestion for Christians is to read your Bible and find all the references that describe how God feels about animals. Schedule a private time when you can read alone, and use a pen and paper to note references. Look at the excerpts you have recorded and forget their specific meaning in the Bible for this moment. Interpret them from within your own personal spiritual beliefs. In this way, your Bible can be a tool that will help you gain a better understanding of how your faith considers the human-pet bond and the value of animal life.

Concerning euthanasia, Christian scriptures define mercy killing to prevent suffering and the pain of terminal illness as an expression of God's love. The act of mercy killing is considered to bestow a personal blessing, although it is acknowledged that the act is an emotionally painful one.

Different denominations interpret parts of the Bible differently. You can use the beliefs that reside deep within you to interpret these scriptures in a beneficial way as well. Use your discretion and be true to yourself.

Hinduism

Ancient Hindu sages marveled at the perpetual recurrence of life—the butterfly egg that grows into a caterpillar, and the caterpillar that becomes a butterfly. The sages reasoned that individual lives must be reborn as part of a constant cycle. One life passes from vegetation to animal, animal to humankind, from one human body to another, up and down the scale of life forms. A pure and changing spirit exists beyond the impermanent material world. It is the unseen source of all life and all things.

Hinduism has numerous deities, all of which are manifestations of the one supreme God, Brahman. The goal of Hinduism is to achieve union with that eternal spirit through ritual, purity, self-control, nonviolence, truth, charity and compassion toward all living creatures.

The Hindus see the universal soul in everything; all life is revered. Most Hindus are vegetarians and practice nonviolence toward animals. Cows especially are revered for the milk and labor they have supplied for centuries, and the consumption of beef is considered sacrilege. It is typical to see a Hindu bowing to all cows he or she passes, or to witness wealthy men opening hostels to house decrepit and elderly cows. Cows wander freely through most Indian cities. Feeding the cows small offerings of food is considered a religious act.

Animals have always held a sacred position in Hinduism. Snakes are partly divine and have a god of their own. Monkeys continue to live in temples honoring Hanuman, the monkey god. Animals are also included in the celebration of sacred holidays. On the holiday of Dewali, elephants participate in the celebration, beautifully painted with natural dyes for the occasion.

The Hindu belief system offers much for the bereaved pet owner. There is sympathy and compassion for those who mourn the death of a beloved pet. The Hindus believe in reincarnation for all living creatures. Every living creature who dies is reborn according to his or her karma. The form of life the spirit will take in rebirth depends upon what the spirit did in past lives, and the form of life it will receive next time depends upon its actions in this life. It is believed that a better rebirth for ancestors and loved ones can be achieved by conducting special rites and pilgrimages.

Ritual, prayer and positive action are recommended to the bereaved. Many Hindus believe in reunion with a loved one in death, and meditating upon this reunion can help the bereaved cope with his or her grief.

Islam

The Holy Prophet used to say, "Whoever is kind to the creatures of God, is kind to himself."[3] The Qur'an emphasizes that the intrinsic value of all animals should be recognized, irrespective of their usefulness or their apparent harmfulness. There is a Hadith about a prophet who was stung by an ant and, in anger, ordered that the ants' nest be burned. At this, God reprimanded the prophet: "Because one ant stung you, you have burned a whole community which glorified Me."

Many passages from the Qur'an and Ahadith state that all animals are endowed with spirit and mind. The Qur'an Majeed states that animals have a cognizance of their Creator and, hence, they pay their obeisance to Him by adoration and worship: "Seest thou not that it is Allah Whose praises are celebrated by all beings in the heavens and on earth, and by the birds with extended wings? Each one knows its prayer and psalm, And Allah is aware of what they do" (Qur'an 24:41). God speaks directly to animals, as the following verse shows: "And your Lord revealed to the bee, saying: 'make hives in the mountains and in the trees, and in (human) habitations' " (Qur'an 16:68). The Qur'an Majeed uses the same Arabic word ("Wahi") for God's revelation to the bee as it uses for His revelation to all His Prophets, including the Holy Prophet Muhammad. Such stories prove that animals have a sufficient degree of psychic endowment to understand and follow God's messages.

The universal mercy of Islam embraces not only humans but all other living creatures of Allah. Kindness to animals is a part of the Islamic faith, and Muslims are required to treat animals humanely. Cruelty to animals is sufficient reason for a person to be thrown into the Fire, i.e., "hell."

Islam holds that a person is responsible for the well-being of a pet and shall be accountable for any negligence and carelessness in this connection. If an animal has terminal illness, after taking all the possible measures to save the animal from pain and suffering, if there is absolutely no hope of success, then many believe the animal should be put to sleep to save it from further suffering and pain.

There are numerous legends about the Muslim saints and holy men who could talk to animals. It stands to reason that spiritual communication with your deceased animal companion would be acceptable to Allah.

Judaism

Judaism, like Christianity, practices a deep concern for the humane treatment of animals, but has no doctrines concerning the human-pet bond. Judaism views all living creatures as God's creation. Humanity has the responsibility to protect and treat them with love.

The Hebrew scriptures demonstrate concern for animals by specifically applying the Sabbath laws of rest to the animal kingdom, and by stating that animals must be kept protected and free from stress and pain.

It is clear that in Judaism strict laws must be followed to fulfill our obligations as animal guardians. Concerning the death of a pet, most of the rabbis I've consulted have nearly the same attitude—there should be sympathy for the grieving pet guardian, careful planning and suitable arrangements for the pet's remains. The deceased pet, having brought life and love to his or her guardian, deserves loving care in death as it had in life. Once the death has occurred, and the proper disposal of the remains made, mourning is respected and accepted but should not continue to excess.

Native American Beliefs

To best understand the Native American Indian viewpoint, we shall examine the Lakota beliefs, which I believe are the most accessible.

In the Lakota sacred language and beliefs, nonhuman species of life are valued as if they were human. Each species of the animal kingdom is appointed to its own "nation," such as the Owl Nation, and relationships between the human and animal nations are recognized. It is believed that companion relationships between animal nations exist as well.

The Lakota see a continuous relationship between nature and culture. They believe that, as the last arrivals to the created earth, humans are the newest, youngest and most ignorant of life forms in the world, and must strive to learn from those who have been here longer. The medicine man or woman obtains this knowledge from animals and other animate and inanimate forms that serve as advisors or helpers. Once the medicine man has received a vision, he may be required to act out his vision publicly and to imitate the animals and birds who communicated with him and gave him power.

To the Lakota, all animate creatures and inanimate objects are interdependent. Therefore, humans are merely another part of the universe, not greater or less than any other life form. Animals, birds, insects, trees, flowers, rocks—all living species are considered on the same level as humans. All have a "soul." In English, the Lakota are often called animists for this reason.

The Lakota believe that all animate beings experience reincarnation, but they do not have a name for the soul as we understand it. They understand rebirth as a process consisting of four states of individualism. William K. Powers, author of *Sacred Language: The Nature Of Supernatural Discourse In Lakota* (Norman, Oklahoma: University of Oklahoma Press, 1986), explains the process using an analogy to the production of fire. The chart below simplifies the understanding of this process.

Lakota Name	Analogy	Definition
Sicun	Spark	Potential for being
Tun	Tinder	Transforming this potentiality through birth into an essence that is independent of the body
Ni	Flame	Providing continuous evidence that this essence exists
Nagi	Smoke	Showing that the essence, independent of the corporeal existence, continues after death

It can be said that the Lakota believe in these four states as four aspects that the soul takes on as it moves through life. At death, the soul is free to be reborn into another organism.

Native Americans believe that death is a natural cycle of life, and is not to be feared. Pet death is understood and accepted as a reality. As with the death of a human loved one, ritual activities and prayer are recommended to assist the departed soul toward reincarnation. Although grief is felt, energies are focused upon ritualistically assisting the soul beyond, and preserving the deceased loved one's memory. Communication with ancestors and deceased loved ones is possible, and death does not mean the end to a loving relationship, but rather a transformation.

Contemporary Paganism

Contemporary paganism encompasses witchcraft, shamanism, revived ancient traditions, earth religions, folk magic, folk medicine and specific occult sciences of positive intent that practice reverence or recognition of nature. Through paganism many have acquired a renewed unity with and appreciation of nature. Practitioners focus reverence upon the cycles of nature and observe kinship with other living creatures. Reviving the ancient human-nature bond helps to direct attention and acceptance toward the human-pet bond.

Reverence for nature coupled with increased environmental awareness offers pet lovers solace, acceptance and hope. Animals, just like humans, are seen as children of the earth. All of nature's cycles and life forms are said to exist in harmony, and this theology of connection includes reunion through death and rebirth through reincarnation. Paganism teaches that animals are beautiful creatures who share this planet with humans and are to be loved, respected and humanely treated. Animals are not ours to exploit. Their environments are to be preserved and their lives cherished.

The pagan religion of Wicca is one of many religions whose deities take a special interest in nature's living creatures. The cat and dog, popular family pets, are two of the numerous creatures associated with the Goddess and God. The deities' domain includes all living creatures, and animals are thought of as akin to humanity, not beneath us. The God and Goddess represent the male and female aspects of nature. The Goddess is the universal mother and is a symbol of eternal wisdom, fertility and nurturing. Life is a gift She gives with the promise of rebirth at death. Most practitioners ask Her for strength, guidance and nurturing during their mourning and coping with a loved one's death. All creatures, pets included, are divine in Her and the God.

Instead of a church or temple, Wiccans practice their religion in covens, which are similar to prayer groups. When a Wiccan who belongs to a coven experiences the tragic loss of a dear animal friend, the coven should recognize the loss in their next meeting, talk with the grieving individual and discuss what help is needed emotionally and spiritually. Discussion should include what the individual wants or needs in order to make the arrangements desired for his or her pet—be it formal burial, home burial or cremation. If the coven member so desires, a ritual can be planned. The coven can decide whether or not to arrange a circle in which magic may be done to assist the beloved's passing soul as it ascends to divinity with the God and Goddess.

Wicca also allows an individual to practice alone, without belonging to a coven. Such Wiccans are called "solitary practitioners." Most have access to fellow practitioners through a network, such as the Internet. A solitary Wiccan should seek out the compassion and interaction with brothers and sisters of the Craft for help with internal healing.

Solitary practitioners of all pagan traditions can formulate their own Crossing the Bridge ceremony or plan their next ritual to include special phrases dedicated to the passing of their beloved pet from the physical plane to the spiritual plane.

Unitarian-Universalism

Unitarian-Universalist churches are gaining popularity in the United States. In this faith, which is based in the spirit of earth-centered religious traditions, animals are brothers and sisters to the human race. The Catholic Saint Francis is respected and often used as a role model for discussion in the church teachings concerning animals.

The Unitarian-Universalist Association teaches as its first principle that each individual has the freedom to decide what is true for him- or herself, and to act according to those beliefs. This in itself relieves any worry people might have that in attending a Unitarian-Universalist service or making use of its tenets they are somehow going against their own religious doctrines.

The second principle states that the dignity and inherent worth of each person is part of the interdependent web of existence. When a Unitarian-Universalist suffers the grief of a pet death, both principles can offer guidance.

Within this web of existence, humans and animals are bound together through love and companionship, and pets are accorded high importance. We humans display our true selves when a pet calls for our attention or when we engage with a pet; therefore pets are seen as beneficial, and the human-pet bond is acknowledged as a real and loving relationship.

The loss a pet guardian feels is considered real and significant, because a strand of the web of existence has been broken. The bereaved must be attended to by the congregation of the church. Other members of the congregation acknowledge the reality of the loss, show compassion and help in relieving the person's emptiness through prayer, meditation exercises, ritual and counseling. Healthy mourning is discussed and practiced. Sharing the grief that the death of a beloved pet brings is encouraged. These exercises are considered positive actions toward resolution and growth.

Every religion considers the phenomena of birth, life, death and some form of rebirth. Most provide some insight into the human-animal bond. The fact that a religious doctrine does not discuss pet care or pet death does not make it unsuitable for your needs at this time. Every spiritual belief system offers some form of enlightenment.

The best enlightenment can be found within you. Armed with your spiritual faith and practices, look within to find truth. Ritual, meditation and positive thought will prompt your healing. You will be granted divine answers and spiritual growth—precious spiritual assets that will serve you for a lifetime.

Afterword

DURING YOUR MOURNING, YOU MAY FEEL EMPTINESS, CONFUSION and stress. Even after the healing and resolution, some questions will remain unanswered and a part of your grief will always exist. Throughout the process, however, try to concentrate on the joyous moments you had with your pet. The love between you and your pet is eternal; consider that you may experience a joyful reunion at your moment of crossing the threshold into the spiritual plane.

No amount of discussion or information can prepare you for the loss of a pet or make your grieving process easier. I understand that and have experienced the sadness and difficulty of pet loss myself. My deepest desire and hope is that this book has made your grieving easier, provided some insight and given you a head start toward resolution.

Always remember that in grief you are not alone—you are experiencing the natural emotions that we all share. Open your mind, look within yourself and pray as an additional method of coping and gaining resolution. Have faith in yourself.

Your love for your pet and his or her love for you will be forever existent in the universe as an energy that never fades.

Notes

Chapter One

1. Sife, Wallace, *The Loss of a Pet*. New York: Howell Book House, 1993, p. 8.
2. Ibid, p. 8.
3. Ibid, p. 9.
4. Ibid, p. 18.
5. Ibid, p. 11.

Chapter Two

1. Sife, p. 24.
2. Ibid, p. 25.
3. Ibid, p. 46.
4. Ibid, p. 32.
5. Ibid, p. 31.
6. Ibid, p. 53.

Chapter Five

1. Cunningham, Scott, *Magical Aromatherapy*. St. Paul, Minnesota: Llewellyn Publications, 1989, p. 82.

Chapter Seven

1. Sife, p. 120.

Chapter Eight

1. Cunningham, p. 114.

Chapter Nine

1. Stapleton, Michael, *The Illustrated Dictionary of Greek and Roman Mythology*, New York: Peter Bedrick Books, 1986, p. 87.
2. Reed, Ellen Cannon, *Invocation of the Gods*, St. Paul, Minnesota: Llewellyn Publications, 1992, p. 214.
3. O'Regan, Vivienne, *The Pillar of Isis*, London: Aquarian/Thorsons, 1992, p. 57.
4. Ibid, p. 57.

Chapter Ten

1. Sife, p. 135.
2. Ibid, p. 136, 137.
3. Muhammad Amin, *Wisdom of Prophet Mohammad*. Lahore, Pakistan: The Lion Press, 1945.

Glossary

Alienation—The feeling of deep disappointment that leads to withdrawal or abstinence from feelings, affections or daily activity. Usually an emotional response that is overcome through the process of grief. If alienation is not overcome in good time, the mourning individual should seek professional assistance.

Altar—Placed in your sacred space, it represents the cosmos, universal energies, the earth, yourself and your spirituality.

Anointing oil—Essential oil used in ritual to anoint participants in blessing or for purification, or used as an aid in shifting consciousness.

Apathy—An absence of feeling that may occur at some point in the grieving process. If this stage is prolonged, professional help may be needed.

Battering—Emotional self-abuse by the grieving individual.

Bereavement—An emotional state resulting from being deprived of a loved one who has died.

Bond—The emotional attachment between yourself and your pet, or yourself and a loved one.

Censer—A fireproof container that holds burning incense. It is usually placed on the right side of the altar; symbolic of the Wiccan God.

Columbarium—A special repository at a pet cemetery for storing the ashes of cremated bodies.

Cremation—A procedure in which the deceased's body is placed upon a heat-safe tray and slid into a large, oven-like structure that burns white-hot. Afterward, the remaining skeleton is ground down into ashes.

Crossing the Bridge ritual—Practitioners of Wicca use this rite to bid farewell to deceased loved ones and assist their crossing the threshold at death into Summerland. I have altered it herein to bid farewell to our animal companions at death.

Deity—A divine being; a god or goddess. Your deity is the supreme being, creator or source of your spiritual beliefs.

Depression—A psychological state of feeling inadequate, overwhelmingly distressed and deeply saddened. Prolonged depression is a signal that professional intervention is needed.

Euthanasia—The procedure of intravenously injecting drugs to induce a pain-free death. It is currently used for animals and death row inmates only.

Fantasy—The act of creating a pleasing mental image to satisfy an inner need.

Freeze-drying—A sophisticated and costly procedure whereby the deceased pet's body is preserved in a desired position.

Humane—Compassionate, respectful and considerate of other life forms.

Obsession—A strong preoccupation that can evolve into an abnormal practice.

Ossuary—A vault or structure at a pet cemetery that contains the bones or ashes of the deceased.

Post-traumatic stress—Exceptional stress due to intense emotional shock.

Self-defeat—Unconsciously undermining one's own objectives, progress or well-being.

Self-recrimination—Blaming oneself for events that could not have been predetermined, controlled or altered.

Sentient—Consciously aware, perceiving and thinking.

Taxidermy—The process of artistically preparing a deceased body, removing the internal organs and stuffing the body. The procedure has many sophisticated steps, and preserving chemicals are used. Taxidermists can also remove an animal's fur in order to preserve the pelt.

Transcendence—Excelling or surpassing usual spiritual limits.

Trauma—A physical, mental or emotional condition, resulting from an intense injury or stress, that can produce disordered behavior and/or feelings.

Unconscious—The mind's functioning that exists beyond the levels of awareness.

Vulnerable—Undefended; left open to possible physical, mental or emotional damage.

Suggested Reading

✿

Pet Bereavement

Bernstein, Joanne, *Loss and How to Cope with It*, New York: Seabury Press, 1977. A guide for juveniles.

Bode, Janet, *Death Is Hard to Live with: Teenagers and How They Cope with Loss*, New York: Delacorte Press, 1993.

Donnelley, Nina Hermann, *I Never Know What to Say*, New York: Ballantine Books, 1987. An excellent guide to helping a grieving friend or family member.

Fitzgerald, Helen, *The Grieving Child: A Parent's Guide*, New York: Simon and Schuster, 1992.

Holmes, Marjorie, *To Help You through the Hurting*, New York: Doubleday, 1983.

Lightner, Candy, *Giving Sorrow Words: How to Cope with Grief and Get on with Your Life*, New York: Warner Books, 1990.

Nieburg, A. Herbert and Fischer, Arlene, *Pet Loss: A Thoughtful Guide for Adults and Children*, New York: Harper and Row, 1982.

Quackenbush, Jamie and Denise Graveline, *When Your Pet Dies: How to Cope with Your Feelings*, New York: Simon and Schuster, 1985.

Sife, Wallace, *The Loss of a Pet*, New York: Howell Book House, 1993. A reference book for this text. Excellent.

**Techniques for Meditation, Chakra Therapy,
Coping and Healing**

These books offer coping and healing techniques that can help with your grief and other emotional challenges in life.

Adair, Margot, *Working Inside Out: Tools for Change*, Berkeley, California: Wingbow Press, 1984.

Finley, Guy, *Freedom From the Ties That Bind: The Secret of Self-Liberation*, Saint Paul, Minnesota: Llewellyn Publications, 1994.

Finley, Guy, *The Secret of Letting Go*, Saint Paul, Minnesota: Llewellyn Publications, 1990.

Harner, Michael, *The Way of the Shaman*, San Francisco: Harper and Row, 1981.

Hope, Murry, *The Psychology of Healing*, Dorset, England: Element Books, 1989.

———, *The Psychology of Ritual*, Dorset, England: Element Books, 1988.

Humphrey, Naomi, *Meditation: The Inner Way*, London: The Aquarian Press, 1987.

Lautie, Raymond and André Passebecq, *Aromatherapy: The Use of Plant Essences in Healing,* Wellingborough, England: Thorsons Publishers Limited, 1979.

Lemesurier, Peter, *Healing of the Gods: The Magic of Symbols and Practice of Theotherapy,* Dorset, England: Element Books, 1988.

Rainwater, Janette, *You're in Charge: A Guide to Becoming Your Own Therapist,* Marina del Rey: DeVorss and Company, 1979.

Tisserand, Robert, *Aromatherapy to Heal and Tend the Body,* Wilmot, Wisconsin: Lotus Press, 1988.

Appendix

Centers for Pet Bereavement Counseling

❧

Listed below are centers where counseling about pet death is available. If none of these locations is convenient for you, write or call them to ask if they can direct you to a resource in your area. If the technology is available to you, look for information on the Internet.

The University of California
School of Veterinary Medicine
One Shields Avenue
Davis, CA 95616
530-752-1393
www.vetmed.ucdavis.edu

The following center was featured on the Arts & Entertainment channel's TV series *Dogs*, and is highly recommended.

The Animal Medical Center
510 East 62nd Street
New York, NY 10021
212-838-8100
www.amcny.org

The University of Minnesota
College of Veterinary Medicine
1365 Gortner Avenue
Minneapolis, MN 55108
612-624-1919